The Early Settlers
Of
Holland Township, N.J.

The Early Settlers of Holland Township, N.J.
Robert H. Peabody

ISBN: 978-1-300-27840-5

The Early Settlers
Of
Holland Township, N.J.

Being the Writings of

'Squire Jesse Sinclair

And Other Historical Documents

Compiled with commentary
By
Robert H. Peabody

Holland Township Historic Preservation Commission
Holland Township, Hunterdon County, N.J.

4

▓ TABLE OF CONTENTS ▓

**Great care has been taken to publish these articles as
they appeared in the newspapers, including
typographical, spelling and grammatical errors.**

▓ ACKNOWLEDGEMENTS ▓

At the risk of omitting one or more persons, I'd like to thank the following volunteers, some of which contributed hundreds of hours of research and editing toward this compilation: Carla Cielo, Robert Peabody, Kathy Sciarello, Annette Worswick, Shirley Wydner, and members of the Holland Presbyterian Church; and Carol Dietrich Macrini for the cover design.

Prime source research was gathered from the Alexander Library at Rutgers, the State Archives, Hunterdon County Historical Society, and the offices of the Hunterdon County Clerk and Surrogate.

Additionally, funding has been made possible in part by the Hunterdon County Board of Chosen Freeholders, through funds administered by the Hunterdon County Cultural and Heritage Commission.

And thanks to the Holland Township Committee for support throughout this project.

This publication is dedicated to the memory of Jesse Sinclair, and to the past, present and future residents of Holland Township.

Lawrence LaFevre, Chairperson
Holland Twp. Historic Preservation Commission
August 2012

▓ INTRODUCTION ▓

Several years ago while tracing the former owners of the property on which I now happily live, I came to a temporary roadblock when the seller in 1897 was Sheriff Ramsey. Since the Sheriff is never a grantee, this breaks the chain of ownership in the deed indexes. Luckily the deed itself referred to the previous owners as the heirs of Jesse Sinclair, Esq. From Jesse back through Samuel Sinclair to John Sinclair who bought it from James and Gertrude Parker (the last owners of the 7,500 acre Barker tract) was an easy task. I was left with a nagging question: 'Who was Jesse Sinclair, Esq.?' At the time I wondered what could have caused Jesse's heirs to lose the farm to a Sheriff's sale. The questions lay dormant until I happened to find and read at the Hunterdon County Library Reference room a copy of a booklet commemorating the 150th anniversary (in the year 2000) of the founding of the Holland Presbyterian Church. Imagine my surprise to see quotes in this booklet from Jesse Sinclair's Memoirs.

Thus began my search for the life of Jesse Sinclair, Esq. Larry Lafevre suggested I contact Church members, Joyce Gamble and Virginia Derbyshire, both of whom helped put the booklet together. Alas, there was no weighty tome containing Jesse's insight on life in the 19th century, only little notes [Jesse's memoirs have recently been located at the Hunterdon County Historical Society]. Joyce Gamble graciously shared these hand-copied remnants with me. One indicated that it had appeared in The Milford Leader (a local weekly newspaper published between 1880 and 1949 when it was purchased by the Delaware Valley News). The search for copies of The Milford Leader led to the Hunterdon County Historical

Society, which has this newspaper on microfilm. Also in their files in the Sinclair family folder they had another of Jesse's articles from the Leader. During the viewing of the microfilm, I discovered a treasure trove. Jesse Sinclair was a prolific writer. Starting in 1880, he was a regular contributor to the "local correspondents" section of the newspaper from the "Hill Regions" writing under the byline of "Musconetcong." In 1892 he began a 24 part series on the "Early Settlers of Holland Township"; followed in 1894 by an 8 part series on the Hunt family; in 1896 by a 5 part series on the "History of Holland prior to the Organization of the Holland Presbyterian Church"; in 1897 (posthumously) by a 4 part series on the history of the "Holland School". In addition to his journalistic efforts, The Milford Leader contains a fair amount written about him. At some point in this information gathering process, I realized that others might find all this of some interest and that it should be republished for my current and future neighbors to have a look into what life was like in 18th and 19th century Holland Township. I am grateful that the Holland Township Historic Preservation Commission has endorsed this assessment and has agreed to publish the manuscript.

Robert H. Peabody
April 2004

Figure 1. Barn on land owned by Jesse Sinclair. Original barn was destroyed by fire in 1878 and rebuilt in 1879. Property is located on Alfalfa Hill Rd. Photo courtesy of Kathy Sciarello. Circa 1915.

■ MISCELLANEOUS NEWSPAPER ARTICLES ■ FROM THE HUNTERDON INDEPENDENT

For The Hunterdon Independent.
Vol. VIII, No. 31
Saturday, Nov. 30, 1878

Holland, N. J., Nov. 26, 1878
    One of the 3d Ward carpenters of Phillipsburg emigrated to Holland on Tuesday last.
    The Bel. Del. R. R. Co. had several hands engaged last week tearing away the old coal house at the station, and removing and repairing the switch; all the old debris has been removed.
    The Presbyterian Sabbath School intend holding a concert in the church in a week or two. They are making preparations for it, and although it is their first attempt, they intend making it a success.
    Mr. David Hart, whose reception was last Tuesday, took his wife to her home in Finesville, on Saturday evening, and as they stopped in front of the house, Mr. H. was in the act of taking a valise out of the wagon, when the horse suddenly turned around and dashed down the street at a fearful rate. The wagon was badly wrecked, but no one was hurt.

About six o'clock on Monday evening, the people of Holland and surrounding country were aroused by the appearance of a large fire on the mountain between this place and Finesville. It was soon discovered to be the barn of Mr. Jesse Sinclair. The fire started in the barrack in the rear of the barn, which was filled with oats. The barn caught fire at about the same time, and was soon in flames. Praise is due to Miss Ella Fisher, a young lady living with Mr. Sinclair, who succeeded in getting one of the horses out before any other assistance arrived. The live stock was all saved, but the machinery and harness were burned. A large wagon house which stood near was saved by the timely arrival of a large number of fire pails, which were kindly brought there by Mr. Benjamin Riegel from his paper mill. The fire lighted the country for miles around, and some three or four hundred people were present, witnessing the sight. Mr. Sinclair was on his way to church at the time, but seeing the light turned back. He had just finished hauling in his cornstalks that day, and they with all the hay and grain were destroyed, except a small quantity of oats, which was taken from the barrickry. The people are at a loss to know who it was, as it is evidently the work of an incendiary. Mr. Sinclair is a highly respected person, and is not known to have an enemy. There is a small insurance.

Figure 2. Another view of the Jesse Sinclair barn. Photo courtesy of the Birkner family. Circa 1930's.

For The Hunterdon Independent.
Vol. VIII, No. 33
Saturday, Dec 14, 1878

Holland, N. J., Dec. 11, 1878

Extra meetings are being held by Rev. G. Tenney in the Finesville Christian Church.

The concert given by the Presbyterian Sabbath School last Sunday evening was good; considering it was their first attempt.

Mr. Wm Sinclair of this place has rented his farm to Mr. Godfrey Bellis, and intends going West in company with some persons of Easton in the Spring.

On Wednesday of last week, as Mr. Wm. Wieder, of Spring Mills, was unloading lime, the leaders became frightened and turned around into the slacked lime, drawing the others with them, and in so doing became entangled in the harness so that it was with great difficulty they succeeded in getting them out. Three of them were so severely burned that it will be necessary to kill them—two of them belonging to Mr. Wieder, and one to a young man living there, the other one was not so badly burned and will do to work in a few weeks. It belonging to Mr. Samuel Britton, who was visiting Mr. Wieders.

For The Hunterdon Independent.
Vol. VIII, No. 34
Saturday, Dec. 21, 1878

Holland

The Durham Iron Co. is building a large flat to be used at the ferry in carrying large cars over the river from the Bel. Del. R. R. to the furnace, so as to save the trouble and expend of rehandling the ore and iron.

The neighbors of Mr. Jesse Sinclair have assisted him in putting up good sheds wherein he can shelter his stock. They have also given him feed and several loads of corn fodder. As winter is at hand, he does not intend rebuilding his barn until spring.

The high water on Wednesday night of last week removed Mr. Peter Rapp's corn-fodder stack bodily about one hundred yards. As it is very inconvenient for feeding

Figure 3. Spring Mills as it appeared in 1860. This area is located at the intersection of Rt. 519 and Church Road. Picture taken from the 1860 Farm Map by Matthew Hughes.

where it now stands; Peter wishes the water would have turned and brought it back.

A well known farmer of this place can boast of two young lambs, the first of the season.

Mr. Johnson White laments the loss of a valuable horse. It was suffering from poll-evil and died from its effects on Wednesday last.

We have learned since last week that Mr. Wm. Weider has killed his horses that were so badly burned in the lime and also that Mr. Britton's horse will have to be killed. It is a great loss and a subscription paper has been circulated to assist him buying a new horse.

THE EARLY SETTLERS OF HOLLAND TOWNSHIP

From: The Milford Leader,   **Whole No. 658**
Thursday October 20, 1892

Early Proprietors of Holland Township.

The title to the lands of the Western division of the province of the State of New Jersey having been vested in Wm. Penn, Gawen Lawrie and Nicholas Lucas, these gentlemen by their indenture bearing date the second day of March 1676, granted and conveyed unto Robert Squib, Sr., and Robert Squib, Jr., one ninetieth part of ninety-one hundredths part, being one property or hundredth part of West Jersey, as tenants in common, in fee. This grant embraced about one half the lands of now Holland township

Again, on the thirtieth day of December 1681 the same grantors conveyed to Robert Squib, Jr., another property or hundredth part of West Jersey, to him, his heirs and assigns forever, which together with the former grant constituted all of the lands of old Holland township, (or nearly so).

And the said Robert Squib, Sr., in and by his deed dated the tenth day of November 1686, granted and released all of his estate and interest in and to the first mentioned property unto the said Robert Squib, Jr., his heirs and assigns forever, thereby leaving the said Squib, Jr., the sole proprietor and owner of Holland township, or nearly so as aforesaid. And the said Robert Squib, Jr., afterward dying, left his will bearing date the seventeenth day of July 1694 therein devising all his lands and tenements, to Nathan Tilson, Jonathan Johnson, and Thomas Saywell, and the survivors of them, in trust to sell the same, etc. (Saywell soon after died).

On the twenty sixth day of January 1706, Nathan Tilson and Jonathan Johnson, the surviving executors and devisees of Robert Squib, Jr., by deeds of lease and release, conveyed to Thomas Byerly, Esq., the aforesaid two properties, said deeds being recorded at Burlington, N. J. in book A A A folio 236, etc.

Whether up to this time any survey of these tracts had actually been made is uncertain, but if not, they were pretty definitely located and well known. Nor does it appear that they were even yet legally surveyed until May 15th, 1714, at which time, after a warrant previously obtained by Thomas Byerly, and placed on record in the Secretary's office the second day of February 1714, Edward Kemp, a deputy surveyor for West Jersey, ran around the said two tracts and found them to contain together 16,565 acres besides allowance for the Musconet-cong Creek. As a matter of interest as well as of information to many, it may be here stated that during the nine year interval between his purchase and the survey, Thomas Byerly made, or had made, what are styled random surveys of his purchase, one of which is here given (as the writer obtained it from Dr Henry Race a few years ago) as follows: Begins at a point 67 chains above the mouth of the Wissahawken Creek (about Milford) thence up the Delaware River to mouth of the Musconetcong Creek (this distance is about 540 chains) thence across the creek's mouth and still by Delaware River 64 chains; thence East 69 chains to a crook of the Musconetcong Creek; thence up the creek following the courses thereof 449 chains; (this point must be near Bloomsbury) thence along the woods South 35 degrees East 296 chains to a white oak marked T. B. (Thomas Byerly) thence South 32 chains; thence South 35 degrees

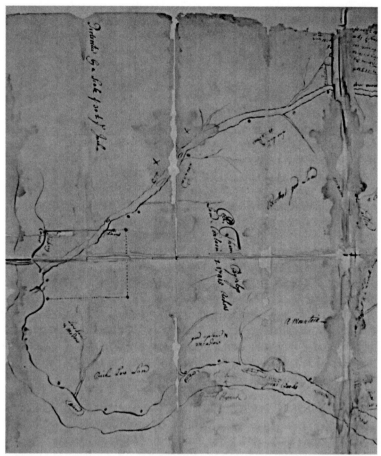

Figure 4. Part of a 1710 map made for Thomas Byerly showing Holland (then Alexandria). Original map located in the James Parker papers, Special Collections and University Archives, Rutgers University Libraries and used with their permission.

West 80 chains to a corner by the side of the Wissahawken Creek; thence down the several courses thereof to Col. Morrls' corner upon said creek near Delaware River; thence due West 52 chains to the side of the river at the place of beginning.

This random survey does not differ very materially from Kemp's except that it don't give as much land in Warren county as we think Kemp does, otherwise the

17

boundaries are nearly the same, the only other difference perhaps being in the line from Bloomsbury to Milford

Jesse Sinclair

[To be continued]

A new stock of breech-loading shot guns just received at Sam'l Sinclair's.
Also the Anthony Wayne and Western Star Washing Machines for $6.00 cash.

**From: The Milford Leader,   Whole No. 659
Thursday October 27, 1892**

Early Proprietors of Holland Township.
[Continued from last week.]

After a while it came to pass that Thomas Byerly also died and left a will bearing date the twenty-sixth day of May 1725, therein devising one property of his estate unto Robert Barker, Esq, of Busbridge, England and the residue of his estate to Joseph Murray and John Kinsey, and the survivors of them, in trust to sell the same, etc. John Kinsey died leaving Joseph Murray the survivor. In pursuance of said Byerly's will the said Robert Barker became seized of the Western property of West Jersey which began at a point commonly called the "Big Rock" on the Delaware River; thence North 48 degrees East 248 chains; thence North 47 degrees West 148 chains to Musconetcong Creek; thence down said creek to Delaware River; thence down said river to the beginning, and containing about 7,500 acres, more or less.

From old deeds we find that one Edward John Bell became legally seized in fee of the said Robert Barker's lands, but when and how we are unable to state, and that being so seized in fee did by his deed bearing date the fourth day of January 1793, grant and convey the same unto James Parker and Gertrude his wife, or the survivors of them, their heirs and assigns forever. This deed is also recorded at Burlington in Book A R. pages 181, etc.

It will be observed that Byerly's lands lying in Warren county form no part of Barker's tract. Hence it was that Charles Williams and Thomas Jones, the executors of

Joseph Murray under his will dated April 26, 1757 (Joseph Murray was an executor of Thomas Byerly) being empowered to sell all his real estate did by their deed dated January 12th, 1771, convey to Israel Pemberton all the lands unsold of the said Thomas Byerly and embracing the lands soon after conveyed by Pemberton to Edward Hunt and others.

Thomas Byerly's other property, now commonly known as the Hamilton tract, began also at the "Big Rock" thence with the Barker line on to the Musconetcong Creek; thence up said creek to a corner Byerly's and New Jersey Societies lands; thence with the line of the same South 35 degrees East 190 chains; thence South 39 degrees West 57 chains; thence South 24 degrees West, thrice crossing Wissahawken Creek 226 chains; thence South 51 degrees West 57 chains to a white oak by the side of said creek; thence South 89 degrees West 23 chains to a point on the Delaware 76 chains above the month of said Wissahawken (probably B. D. R. R. Co's wood lot above Milford) thence up the river to the beginning, containing 7,308 acres.

Whether Joseph Murray, the surviving executor of Thomas Byerly sold this tract in his lifetime, or whether Murray's executors, Williams and Jones sold it along with Byerly's other lands in Warren county on the 12th of January 1771, the writer has not ascertained. However some of the older deeds inform us that William Allen and Joseph Turner, of Philadelphia, sometime after the death of Byerly became seized of this tract, and that they, the said William Allen and Joseph Turner, sold and conveyed the said tract to James Hamilton, of Bush Hill, in the county of Philadelphia; and that James Hamilton died and left his will bearing date March 4th, 1776, devising this tract to his nephew, James Hamilton, of the city of Philadelphia, being just one hundred years and two days after the first grant made to Robert Squib in 1676.

We have thus rapidly sketched the freehold and ownership of the described lands for a period of one hundred years. Of course many had up to this time purchased small tracts and settled In Alexandria, of which Holland was then a part, and still more who were renters, but of some of these we may perhaps say more at some future time.

Jesse Sinclair

19

Figure 5. Genealogical Society of New Jersey. Map
Series #4. Sheet C. Hunterdon County. Manuscript
map by D. Stanton Hammond. 1965.

From: The Milford Leader,   Whole No. 661
Thursday, November 10, 1892

Early Settlers of Holland Twp. Continued

Prior to the time when these lands fell into the
hands of James Parker and Gertrude his wife, and James
Hamilton, they had been held in one or at most two tracts
by nonresident owners who were unwilling to sell them in
tracts, the result of which was that most of the early
settlers were compelled to enter upon them under lease or
not at all. Although this state of things no doubt had a
tendency to discourage immigration to this section, yet we
find that considerable settlements must have been made
at a comparatively early period—1750 to 1760, since the
people had become so numerous at some early period as
to require the erection of a blacksmith shop on top of the
Musconetcong Mountain on land then occupied by Jacob
Vanderbilt, now the Eastern edge of Capt. Hart's farm
(which at that period was part of the Vanderbelt tract). In
the beginning of the present century the hearth, old
scraps of iron, horse shoes, nails and other debris
common to blacksmith shops were still visible—also
nearby were the foundation walls of what appeared to
have been at one time a house. Who lived there and
worked in that shop is not known. As before stated, the
title to the Barker tract having in 1793 vested in James
Parker and Gertrude Parker, and the title to the other
tract passed to James Hamilton at or near the same
period, these gentlemen divided their respective lands into
farms or lots to suit purchasers , and so offered to sell
them to their tenants or others wishing to buy them, and
so rapidly did they sell that in ten years thereafter the title
to nearly all of them had passed to bona fide settlers and
so have since remained.

Our object in further writing upon this subject
from time to time will be to rescue from the dim ages of
the past, so far as able, the names of the earlier as well as
the later settlers and owners of the lands within the
bounds of our more immediate neighborhood, being in the
Northwestern part of the township, together with some
description of them and their families when anything
worthy of mention is known. But in doing these things we

shall have to depend more on memory and tradition than on record; the latter not being to any great extent within our reach. This want of records will necessitate the omission of dates to a very great extent—so essential to writings of this kind—and also greatly increase liability to err in our statements, a thing we shall strive to avoid as much as possible under these adverse circumstances. And now we stand upon the bank of the Delaware river at Johnson's Ferry wondering what we shall say or where to begin the first thought that rises up within us. We stand here seventy-five years too late. The beginning of things is greatly obscured amid the dimness of the past ages, and we cannot clearly see them. But on the principle of "Better late than never," we proceed to say that the first settler at or near this point known to us was Jonathan Cornell, who owned about forty acres of land and probably established the ferry. Although the present entering and landing at the Jersey shore is now a few feet outside the line of Cornell's land yet it could easily have been within it at that early date, and afterward changed to its present site by Thomas Purcel who in 1793 or 94 probably bought Cornell's ferry rights and 190 acres of land adjoining the same. After this period the ferry was owned by Purcel and called by his name till about 1804 when he sold his ferry rights with 52-1/2 acres of his 190 acre tract to Hart Johnson, since which it has been known by the name of Johnson's Ferry. It was much used for ferrying purposes till the building of the bridge at Riegelsville in 1837, when it fell into disuse. In connection with the ferry Mr. Johnson carried on farming, storekeeping and also kept a hotel which business he pursued till his death in 1844. Mr. Johnson probably came to this place from Readington, this county. He was married and had children—Henry W., Elizabeth and Amy. Amy married Jerry King, and Elizabeth William Hartpence. Both of them moved out of the Township. Henry W. always resided in the Township. He owned at one time the Gibson House in Milford, and kept hotel. He followed droving and took great delight in fine horses. He was thrice married and was the father of Dr. John Johnson long settled at Kintnersville, Pa., and grandfather to Dr. Henry W. Johnson, now of Riegelsville, Pa, who bears his name.

Jesse Sinclair

P.S.—The name Bell in last article two weeks ago should have been Ball

—————————————————Tuesday's Election
The election in Holland Township on Tuesday passed off quietly and 447 votes were polled out of 498 on the register

**From: The Milford Leader,   Whole No. 662
Thursday November 17, 1892**

Early Settlers of Holland Twp. Continued

After the death of Hart Johnson, John Tomson bought his place, who with his nephew John T. Fine, carried on for a time much the same business as Mr. Johnson had done. In the year 1849 Mr. Tomson donated and deeded the land on which the Holland Presbyterian Church building stands and what is now called the old part of the cemetery. He was instrumental in the building of the church and was a corporate trustee. He was born Oct. 21 1786 and died May 2d 1867. He married Catharine Fine who was born May 20 1792 and died Nov. 25, 1854 without issue.

The remainder of Thomas Purcel's 190 acre tract with the exception of 26 acres sold to Wm. Moore was not sold until after his death in -----. Prior to the building of a saw mill at the foot of Lyn's falls Abner Welch farmed the land. Welch was succeeded by Christopher Tinsman. After Tinsman moved there Garner A. Hunt claimed the place as one of his preaching stations. On one occasion Mr. Hunt, wearied with his ride, stopped at Hart Johnson's to refresh himself with a little of his good liquor before preaching but on arriving at the station the old man couldn't navigate himself quite straight and preaching was postponed for four weeks.

After Purcel's death the land was sold partly to Wm. Moore and partly to Wm. Tinsman. Present owners Tlnsman's heirs and Edward Hager.

Soon after his 190 acre purchase, Thomas Purcel bought 233 acres on the Delaware at and near the mouth of the Musconetcong Creek of which we shall say more hereafter.

Some time between the years of 1802 and 1806, Jonathan Cornell sold his fifty acre lot to one John Fisher. After this we hear no more of Cornell. Cornell had built a house and other buildings, if he had any, on the lower edge of this tract. But after Fisher bought it he built a house at the upper edge, which was known and still remembered by many yet living as the red house. Not far from the year 1820, perhaps before, John Bloom purchased the Fisher land and as we now think lived in this house for a time, and then built himself another house, barn and other building's again at the lower side. This house was afterwards carried away or destroyed by the big Delaware freshet the eighth of January 1841. He then built another house farther back from the river which is still standing, and at present owned and occupied by Lewis U. Bloom. Mr. Bloom was a carpenter by trade; but he appears to have been a good farmer as well. At the time of his death he had acquired in addition to his first purchase most of the Brink lands, and twelve-fifteenths of the old John Moore tract and was considered a man well to do in his day. He contributed liberally toward the Holland Presbyterian Church, took an active part in its building and was one of its first trustees. John Bloom was the son of Herbert Bloom who had at some early day settled on the Musconetcong Mountain. He was born Sept. 22d, 1793 in a house that stood at that time a short distance East from the old Alexander Brodhead buildings. He was a brother to Jacob Bloom, the father of Wm. V. Bloom, of Little York, also a brother to the wife of Alexander Brodhead, the mother of John Brodhead, of Milford. He married Hannah Brink who was born at Durham Ferry, June 21, 1800. They had children, sons— Daniel, John D., Henry, William, Jacob, Lewis U. and David R. Daughters—Mary, Ann, Matilda, Lizzie and Amy. They all married, and except Henry, all are living, the youngest somewhere between 40 and 50 years. They have all moved away from the township except Lewis U. at the old homestead, and Amy, the wife of George W. Hager. John Bloom died in his home February 24, 1865, and Hannah, his wife, January 6, 1875. They were buried in Holland cemetery.

It would be interesting to trace the lineage of this and other families down to the present, but the limits of newspaper articles forbid it. We therefore bid good by to them at a period of from fifty to seventy-five years ago.

Jesse Sinclair.

Hard to beat (as persons attest who have had them several years hand run) the tap sole boot Sailer & Farrand are selling at $2.00.

From: The Milford Leader   Whole No. 663
Thursday November 24, 1892

Early Settlers of Holland Twp. Continued

We are now at Durham's Ferry. This is on the Delaware about half a mile above Johnson's Ferry. Prior to 1800 it was called Stillwell's ferry; after the name of the man who lived there at that time. This is no doubt correct, as the writer has frequently heard John Bloom speak of Stillwell, who lived here before Daniel Brink. But if the ferry is as old as Durham furnace, there must have lived some one here before Stillwell; and he is the man we should like to find, but now fear we shall never be gratified in this respect. However in 1779, Daniel Brink succeeded Stillwell at this place. Whether a hotel had been kept here before Brink came to it we do not know but rather think there may have been. But whether or not, Daniel Brink obtained a license that same year he moved to it, and kept a tavern at it until his death in 1826-7. After Mr. Brink's death a tavern was still kept here by the following persons: Jacob Snyder, Joseph R. Allen, Wm. Runyon, Jacob Snyder, John R. Pinkerton, Wm. H. Heller and Wm. Runyon, the last in 1833-4, making in all eighty four consecutive years. Since then there has been no tavern here. It is now owned by Silas M. Wolfinger. Besides being a ferry, the place has a good eddy in which to land rafts and was much used in early days for that purpose. Whether Skinner and Parks who engineered the first raft on the Delaware through from Cochecton to Philadelphia in 1746 stopped over night at this place is not certain, nor yet improbable, since Durham on account of its iron works must have been widely known even in that early day.

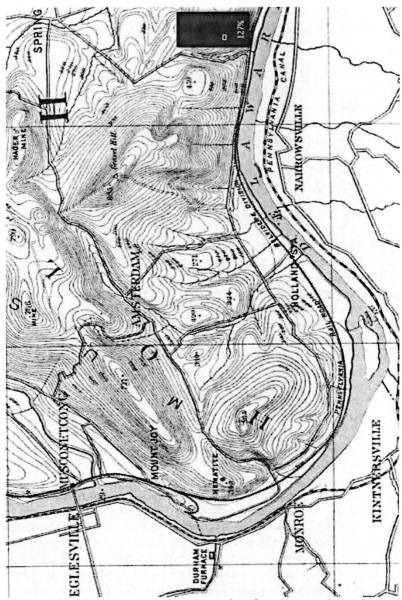

Figure 6. 1885 map showing the ferry crossing the Delaware at the Durham Furnace. Taken from A Topographical Map of the Southwestern Highlands by G. Cook, J. Smock and C. C. Vermeule.

Daniel Brink married Mary Rockafellow and had children—John, Henry, Daniel, Hannah and Matilda. John and Henry moved away from here when young. Daniel died unmarried. Hannah married John Bloom and Matilda Wm. Welch. Mrs. Welch is still living in her eighty-third year.

Adjoining the ferry is, or was, a tract of 100 acres now owned in parcels by Wm. Zearfoss, Cooper and Hewitt, and Sherred Tinsman. The first settler on this tract was probably John Allen. He was on it in 1794, probably much earlier. John Allen was a surveyor. In 1779 (typo. actually 1799-Ed.) he surveyed John Sinclair's lands which survey was filed in the Supreme Court, Trenton, N. J., in the matter of John Sinclair's application to that court to supply the loss of his title deed which had been destroyed in the burning of his house in that year. Some time after 1806 Michael Zearfoss bought of Allen this tract, and afterwards sold a part of it to Henry Quin, who built at Durham falls a saw-mill and grist-mill. These mills burned down in 1847. Mr. Quin did not rebuild. The saw-mill, however, was afterward rebuilt by Thomas P. Tinsman.

Figure 7. Residence and sawmill of Thomas P. Tinsman. Picture taken from the 1860 Farm Map by Matthew Hughes.

Mr. Quin was quite a genius. He invented a corn kiln and dryer, much superior to any in use before; also self-setting works for saw-mills; also published a book neither of which paid him. He was of Irish descent. Married Rachel Williams, had children—George, Emmet, Isaac, Robert, Sarah, Ann, and Rachel. They have all long since moved away except Sarah, who married John C. Britton, and Rachel, who married Daniel Purcel. These at present live in Milford.

Michael Zearfoss before mentioned was a German both as to birth and education. He was married. His children were: Michael, George, Mary and others we never knew. Michael married Susan Fishler, George Elizabeth Price and Mary, Wm. Sinclair. Soon after Michael Zearfoss purchased the above tract he appears to have sold a small part of it to his son Michael. This part still bears the name of Zearfoss, being at present owned by Wm. Zearfoss a grand child of the first mentioned Michael. Mrs. Jane Pursel also sustains the relation of a grand child to him.

We next step into Mt. Joy, Phillip Lippencott was probably the pioneer in this place. He had at an early period a house built to live in, and another to teach school in. He taught here many years. He was also a commissioner of deeds and done conveyancing and kept a candy shop. He was born about 1800; when a child had white swelling and ever after walked on crutches. He died about 20 years ago. At our last visit to Mt. Joy in 1889 it contained several dwellings, had a saw-mill, two stores, barber shop, carpet factory and harness shop.

Jesse Sinclair.

November 17, 1892

A good variety of horse blankets, wolf and plush robes at A. S. Eckel's hardware store, Milford,NJ

**From: The Milford Leader,   Whole No. 664
Thursday, December 1, 1892**

Early Settlers of Holland Twp. Continued

Mount Joy is situated in the South West corner of Thomas Purcell's 233 acre tract heretofore mentioned, the latter part of which we shall next speak. This tract resembles in shape that of a boot, and extends from Mt

Joy to formerly Phillip Fine's land, a distance of about one and a quarter miles. Who settled on it before Purcell we do not know. He probably bought it of James Parker sometime before 1800, at all events, in the beginning of the present century, he built upon it two saw-mills, one at the mouth of the Musconetcong Creek, the other half a mile further up the creek. He himself operated the lower mill and rented the upper one if our memory serves us correctly to Edward Welsted. The mills done a good business in their day. After Purcell's death in 1827, Edward Welsted, John Duckworth and Wilson Housel were appointed commissioners to make divisions of the land, which they did as follows: first set off about 115 acres together with the mansion house and other buildings thereto, to the use of the widow, as, and for her thirds therin; next 10 or 12 acres attached to the lower mill, and 105 acres attached to the upper mill. On the 27th of February 1828, the said commissioners, at the house of James Smith, innkeeper at Spring Garden in Alexandria, sold the upper mill and lands to Peter Tinsman and Hugh Major; the lower mill and lot to Benjamin Riegel, (farmer,) and his unsold lands below Johnson's Ferry to Christopher Tlnsman, (and not to Moore and Tlnsman as before stated, they obtained them afterward), Edward Llppencott lived on and farmed the widow's land until her death. In 1881 Hugh Major and Maria his wife released their rights in the upper mill and land to Peter Tinsman, who carried on the farming and lumbering business here for several years and then sold the property to Nelson Angel, who drove on the business for some years and sold it to Benjamin Riegel (present owner). The mill has ceased to be. The lower mill was run by Jessie Riegel until 1844, when Isaac T. Riegel bought it, and the dower land which came into market about that time and worked them both for about forty years and then sold them to Benjamin Riegel the present owner, the mill having previously burned down.

Of what nationality Thomas Purcell was, or when born we do not know. He appears to have first settled at Monroe, Pa prior to 1780 and bought, it is said, 176 acres of land; first erected thereon a log house, then a saw-mill, and afterward built a second mill. About 1790, or soon thereafter, he sold out at Monroe and came to New Jersey, and bought lands and built mills, as herein and heretofore

described. He was married and had eight daughters—
Mary, Maria, Jane, Ruth, Eliza, Nancy and two others
whose names we do not recall. Mary was married to Peter
Tinsman, Maria to Hugh Major, Jane to Edward
Lippencott, Ruth to Samuel Eichlin, Eliza to Joseph Raub.
Nancy never married. Of the unremembered ones, one
married John Dillon, and the other a Gordon. Purcell was
buried in an old grave yard on the farm of the late John M.
Smith. Wm. Lippencott, Samuel, Archibald and James
Eichlin are his grandchildren living In Holland. Tomson
Fine is his great grandchild. Dr. John C. Purcell was a
descendent of his.

Adjoining Purcell's lands at the place was a farm of
about 93 acres of which one George Helms had become
seized, but at what time or how, the writer does not know.
Probably in or about 1821 George Helms conveyed his
lands to Peter Fraley, who lived on and farmed them until
his death in 1874. In 1876 Peter Fraley's heirs at law
conveyed to his widow, Mary Fraley, a life interest in a
house and lot being a part of said lands and premises and
at the same time conveyed the remainder thereof to
Joseph Fraley. In 1882 Joseph Fraley died. The following
year after his death the property was sold to Benjamin
Riegel. Mr. Riegel has since erected on it a reservoir from
which, by means of heavy iron pipe, spring water is
carried to his Paper Mill at Riegelsville, a distance of about
one mile. The water thus brought for use in the mill is
available in case of fire. Peter Fraley was a son of Michael
Freolick and was married to Mary Pippenger. They had six
children. Margaret was married to Richard Hulsizer,
Halena to Wm. Zearfoss, Elizabeth to William Hager, Maria
to Geo. Laubach, Hetty to Albert Opdycke, and Joseph
who married Mary Hartsel, by whom he had four
children—Peter, Charles, Joseph and George. After
Joseph's death his widow with her four little children went
to Nebraska where she has since died.

Jesse Sinclair

Nov. 24, 1892

For the correct styles in Fall derby hats go to W. S.
Smith's

An article published Dec 8, 1892 in The Milford Leader is
missing from this series. No extant copies of this issue
have been found to date, however, the following letter

refers to it and gives at least some of the subject matter [Ed.]

From: The Milford Leader
Thursday , June 7, 1894

Continued History of the Fine Family
Maxon, Osage Co., Kan., May 30, 1894

My friend and old acquaintance, Jesse Sinclair, has been writing concerning grandfather Fine's family and his brother John Fine, but as he does not say anything about his sisters or to whom they were married, I will here state that one of them married John Carpenter, another Isaac Shipman, another George Brackley, another Godfrey Insley, and the youngest I think, married Jeremiah Wilson. I have seen them all at different times at grandfather Fine's where they often came visiting while I was young. I have heard grandmother Fine say that her and grandfather Fine were cousins but I do not know in what way unless her mother was a sister to great grandfather Fine. Her name before she was married to grandfather Fine was Catharine Mellick. She had five brothers, John, William, Christopher, Jacob and Henry, and one sister Margaret who married a man by the name of Hulsizer whose first name I cannot now recall. They had five sons, Martin, Godfrey, William, Daniel, James, that I was acquainted with, and four daughters. One daughter married William Smith, the father of John M. Smith; another married one Drake, the father of John Drake, the wholesale merchant, of Easton; another married Peter Tinsman, a brother of Daniel and William Tinsman; another married John Duckworth. I often saw them at grandfather Fine's when I was young and up to the date of his death which occurred in September 1834. On April 28, the following year, (1835) I became 21 years of age. I do not know that I have any more to write concerning the Fines but will write of the Mellick's in my next.

I was very sorry to hear of the death of cousin Luther Mellick Fine, at Reading. He is one I had never saw as he was born a few years after I moved to Wisconsin.

Note.- There was a mistake in my former letter that I wish to correct. The types made it read that grandfather Fine married Lizzie Zigler. This is wrong. He married a

Mellick. It was great grandfather Fine that married Miss
Zigler.   P. A. F.

From: The Milford Leader   **Whole No. 887**
Thursday, March 25, 1897

Concerning the Fine Family
Scranton, Pa, March 15th, 1897
Editor Milford Leader
Dear Sir:—Referring to an article in The Leader for Dec.
8th, 1892, which I have only recently seen, written by Mr.
Jesse Sinclair, regarding the early settlers of Holland
township: Among other things in speaking of the Fine
family the article states that Andrew M. Fine married Mary
Hartpence and that Mr. Sinclair could not recall the
names of any children except John M., but that they are
all deceased.

        In this connection I beg to advise that all of the
children of Andrew M. Fine are not dead. His children
were named (in order of ages) Isaac, John M., Catharine,
William S., Margaretta, Martin Luther. Of these Isaac,
John M., and Catharine are deceased. William S.,
Margaretta, and Martin Luther, are living.

        John M. Fine married Rachel Carter who is still
living at Finesville as are her children, Charles C.,
Spencer, and Anna, as Mr. Sinclair's article stated.

        William S. Fine is unmarried and resides at
Scranton, Pa.

        Margaretta Fine married S. T. Dickinson, of
Belvidere, N.J., who is engaged in the hardware business
in New York city and lives at Lehighton, Pa. They have two
children living, Florence A. and Horace N. Dickinson, who
is a special insurance agent for the states of Pennsylvania,
Maryland, and Delaware.

        Martin Luther Fine married Limella Chambers, of
Belvidere, N.J., resides in Scranton, Pa, and is Shipping
Agent for the Coal Sales Department of the Delaware &
Hudson Canal Co., with headquarters at Carbondale, Pa.
Their only child, the undersigned, is thus a grandson of
the Andrew M. Fine mentioned in the article and is his
namesake. He is with the D. & H. C. Co., Coal Sales Dept.,
Scranton, Pa.
        Yours very truly,
                Andrew M. Fine

From: **The Milford Leader**   **Whole No. 666**
Thursday, Dec. 15, 1892

The Fine Family Continued.

By way of preface to this letter we remark that the subject to whom it originally related, is Andrew Fine Derr, a son of John Derr whom some of us well remember as the young man who in 1834 came into this part of Alexandria (now Holland) and took from it one of its Fine daughters to be his wife; and who subsequently was the builder of the bridges that span the Delaware at Milford and Frenchtown, NJ. In relation to this subject the *Luzerne Legal Register* says that: "Reupp, in history of Pennsylvania Germans, says that a ship was driven into the capes of the Delaware by stress of weather in 1704 which had intended to go to New York with its ship load of immigrants, who proposed to settle in that State. Among those people was supposed to be Phillip Fein the ancestor of the Fein family, who in common with many of the other people of the ship, started over land from Philadelphia to cross the then unknown wilds of Northern New Jersey to reach New York. Having reached the banks of the Musconetcong river, in what is now Hunterdon county, NJ, Mr. Fein with his brother John, appreciating the advantages of the stream as a water power and the fertility of the soil determined to settle there instead of pursuing the forest which then covered the whole country. Mr. George Brakeley White, of Cumberland, Maryland, in his chronicles of the Brakeley family says that when his ancestor arrived in 1705 on the Musconetcong he found the Fein family already established there. The following is taken from his narrative. The first Phillip Fein settled upon the tract of land where Finesville has since been built, about the year 1700. Like all the early German land holders in this locality he held his estate by virtue of an Indian title, which was subsequently confirmed to his sons Phillip and John by the Lords proprietors. This son Phillip, who married for the second time in 1805 Mrs. Brakeley, and who gave his daughter Catharine in marriage to young Mr. Brakeley, was born July 15, 1744. He was a man of wealth and influence in those early days. His name, as well as that of his brother John, appears

amongst the signers of the constitution of the St. James
Lutheran Church, of Greenwich, NJ, (commonly known as
the Straw Church, on account of the first edifice having
been thatched with straw) in 1770; and he ever took a
deep interest in its welfare. His business ventures were
fortunate. He erected a dam on the Musconetcong river
and built an oil mill, a grist mill and a saw mill. They
were the largest mills in Lopatcong (the general name for
the district) and the earliest of which there exists
authentic accounts. Mr. Fein died September 4, 1810 and
was buried in the Straw Church grave yard. His sons
inherited this valuable property and for many years
conducted and extensive business in grain. His son John,
born in 1767, died in 1826, married Ann Catharine
Mellick, daughter of Captain Andrew Melick, and became
the father of a large family, of which the youngest child
was Hannah Fein, mother of Andrew F. Derr. In common
with many of the early settlers of New Jersey the Feins
and Melicks were slave holders. Though the negroes were
held as slaves, yet they appear to have been accorded a
very much larger measure of freedom than was given such
persons in the South, and even after they were freed, by
either operation of the law or voluntarily by their masters,
they continued to live on the lands of their former masters
and worked for wages for them. Mrs. Hannah Derr had
many childish reminiscences to narrate of this old black
men Caesar and Pompey, who were freedmen in her
father's household in her childhood days. – *Luzerne Legal
Register*, June issue, 1887.

**From: The Milford Leader,   Whole No. 667
Thursday, December 22, 1892**

Early Settlers of Holland Twp. Continued

At the beginning of these sketches it was stated
that in the writing thereof we would have to depend
mainly on memory drawn from personal observation and
tradition. It is quite obvious that it will not be safe to
venture too far out in the woods or we'll get swamped. We
therefore halt on our march Eastward at the place of the
residence of formerly John Fine; and thence South up the
public road to "Mud Fort," gathering up whatever of

interest we may chance to find on our way thitherward. The first place that attracts our attention is a tract of 782 acres on which Alexander Brodhead was early settled and on which he lived until the close of his long life. Mr. Brodhead's predecessor at this place was probably Herbert Bloom. Mr. Bloom's house, which we can yet well remember, stood on this tract, and which from its appearance must have antedated any of Brodhead's buildings by several years. There was a tradition that Mr. Bloom when young had mills in Sussex and was well off, but afterward became reduced and settled here.

Mr. Brodhead was a millwright, which trade he pursued all his life, leaving the affairs of his farm to the care of his boys when they were yet quite young. We have heard it said that Mr. Brodhead was connected with the Brodheads at the Water Gap, whence he came. He was married to Mary, daughter of Herbert Bloom, and had children, sons—John, Herbert and Jacob; daughters— Mary, Susan, Elizabeth and Sarah Ann. John was married to Catharine Welch, Jacob to Miss Bissey, Mary to Edward Haggerty, Susan to John Vanderbelt. Elizabeth and Herbert never married.

Adjoining Brodhead on the East is another farm which contains a cavern in which some British soldiers spent a part of the Winter of 1776-7, who, as tradition says, had left the Royal Army then quartered at New Brunswick, N. J. on a foraging expedition, and who being tempted to the rich lands of Greenwich, were pursued by a squad of militia commanded (probably) by Captain John Maxwell and driven down the Pohatcong creek to Carpentersville, where they crossed the Delaware into Pennsylvania, whence they fled down the shore of the river to the mouth of the Musconetcong, re-crossed again into New Jersey and thence to this cavern.

We next pass Samuel Burgstresser's farm, but we don't know much about its early history. Our fathers used to call it the old Zeke Morris place. In the beginning of the nineteenth century some others owned it, but we have forgotten the name. The first authentic knowledge the writer has of this place was obtained when John Haggerty bought it about sixty years ago. Mr. Haggerty, as will be remembered, was humped shouldered on account of spinal injuries received when young, and had with his mother, two younger brothers and one sister, previously emigrated from Nockamixon, Bucks county, Pa, and first settled on the place where the soldiers had wintered, and where for some time he worked at shoemaking, and his mother at flax spinning, at which she was an expert, until he married, when he bought this old Morris place on which he and his wife and mother worked like beavers at shoemaking, farming and spinning, until about 1850, when he sold it to Phillip Huff, and moved to Warren county and thence back to Nockamixon whence he came, since which we had lost sight of him for forty years, when again we chanced to hear of him through "Battle's" history of Bucks county, Pa, as follows:

Jacob Haggerty was born in Warren county, New Jersey, Sept 22d, 1838, and is a son of John and Catharine Haggerty, natives of New Jersey. His grandfather James Haggerty, came from Ireland, and settled in Nockamixon township. Jacob Walters, his maternal grandfather, came from Germany and settled at the Forge, Warren county, N. J. John Haggerty was a shoemaker and also farmed in New Jersey until 1852, after which he settled in Nockamixon township. He was the father of ten children Mary M., James, Jacob, Sarah E., Solomon W., Annie C., Sophia J., John W., Hannah M., and Preston W. Those deceased are James, Sarah and Solomon. Solomon died of brain fever while serving in the late war. Jacob Haggerty remained with his parents until he was 21 years old. He taught school for eight months, then hired with Jacob B. Snyder, at Plumsteadville, to run his commission Wagon and farm. After remaining there three years, he rented the commission business of Mr. Snyder for one year, then went West one year, and on his return bought out the business of Mr. Snyder which he carried on for ten years. In the meantime he purchased the farm on which he now lives. He sold the commission business to his brother Preston W. In 1883 he was elected County Treasurer and served three years satisfactorily. In I865 he married Mary Landis, of New Britton, by whom he had three children, Maggie, Clara and an infant son. Maggie and the son are deceased. Mr. and Mrs. Haggerty are members of the Presbyterian Church. Mr. Haggerty is and always has been a very popular and influential man.

Jesse Sinclair

Dec 15, I892

36

Candy! Candy! W. S. Smith's is headquarters for candy.

From: The Milford Leader,   **Whole No. 668**
Thursday, December 29, 1892

A good variety of horse blankets, wolf and plush robes at
A. S. Eckel's hardware store, Milford,

Early Settlers of Holland Twp. Continued

This is "Mud Fort." It was said that Samuel
McGloughen gave the place its name from the
circumstance of his having fallen near by into deep mud,
from which he was not able, without help to extricate
himself, and who, upon being liberated, declared the place
perfectly secure from foreign invasion, its mud being a
complete defense. Samuel had been over to Wm. Fine's
still house.

It is here we next find a tract of land of about 250
acres on which one Phillip Bellis was early settled. He was
probably amongst the earliest of Barker's tenants on the
Musconetcong Mountain and afterwards bought the lands
of James Parker. He was twice married; by his first wife he
had a son whose name was Phillip; by his second wife
another son named Herbert, and one daughter, Elsie.
Whether he had other children by either wife we cannot
say, but think it probable he may have had. We remember
very well his second wife -the old grandmother of *all* as
she was called, to distinguish her from her step son
Phillip's widow who also in course of time had become a
grandmother too, and with whom she always lived, rather
than with her own son Herbert, for the reason we suppose
that it was the homestead and her right of dower in some
way lay there. The old Phillip Bellis was said to have been
a large and strong man, and was one of the men from
Hunterdon county that once went about thirty miles up in
Sussex to help some pioneer settlers up there raise their
first frame houses. After his death his two sons, Phillip
and Herbert appear to have held his lands, whether by
inheritance in whole or in part, or by purchase, we don't
know. Phillip was married to Sallie ____ by whom he had
six daughters—Mary, Elsie, Hannah, Mahala, Julian, and
Nancy. If he had any sons we never heard of them. Mary

was married to John Souders, Elsie to Jacob Stoll, Hannah became the first wife of John Butler and Nancy his second wife, Mahala married Wm. Butler and Julian John Wieder. About 50 years ago and after the decease of all grandmothers, John Butler bought the homestead on which he lived until his death about two years ago. About 35 years ago John Butler planted the first peach orchard ever set in this section excepting one set by Enos Clark 47 years ago. John Butler afterward set other orchards, but was successful in the first planted one only. John Butler was the father of thirteen children. Phillip, twice married, first to Anna Angel, second to Hannah Strawn; William married to Matilda Case, Sallie to Wm. Ferris. Jane to Samuel Eichlin, Elizabeth to Henry White, Martha to Erwin Huff, Mahala to Edward Cope, Lemuel to Louisa Commerford, Margaret and James are unmarried. Albert was drowned in the Missouri River, and two died in infancy. As before mentioned, Herbert Bellis, after the death of his father, became the owner of a part of this 250 acre tract, which he successfully managed and lived on until his death, after which he was succeeded by his son John C. Bellis, who is the present owner. It is perhaps worthy of mention that lands are seldom kept in a family for a period of so nearly a hundred years without having passed out of the hands of the second owner. Herbert Bellis was married to Charetta Creveling and had children as follows: Mary who was married to William Vanderbilt, Charetta to John P. Quick, Peter to Lydia Ann McPeck, Phillip to Rosanna Sailor, John C. to Catharine Hawk, Elsie to John Hager, Harriet to Thatcher Hart and Hummer who was killed by lightning while attending school at the old eight square house in Holland about sixty years ago. Of the family yet living we find the names of Harriet, John C and Charetta-the latter being over ninety years old. Elsie, daughter of Phillip the first, was married to Jacob Stoll. In 1802 Jacob Stoll bought 102 acres of land of Jacob Vanderbilt on which he lived till his death which occurred sometime before 1818. They had two children Jacob and Henry-may have had others. As we shall have occasion to refer to Jacob Stoll in our next, we shall say nothing further of him now.

Beside the Bellis land just considered, there is a lot (now the late John P. Quick's) on which one Daniel S. Moore was settled at a comparatively early period. He was in some way connected with the Bellis family either by the marriage of another daughter of Phillip the first, or a daughter of Jacob Stoll—most probably the latter. The old people called him the school teacher and lawyer. He had placed his name, either as principal or surety on a promissory note, drawn in favor of Thomas Stewart for $225, in consequence of which John Cavanaugh, Sheriff of Hunterdon county, sold his lot in the year 1821. What became of him afterwards we do not know.

Jesse Sinclair

Dec 22, 1892

Notice to Trespassers.
All persons are forbid trespassing or hunting on the premises of the undersigned under penalty of the law.

Samuel Burgstresser	M. W. Angel
Samuel Eichlin	W. J. Kitchen
Forman H. Bellis	Howard Lear
William Phillips	F. M. Hager
G. W. & M. Hager	Wm. Mitchnor
R. & W. Burgstresser	James Eichlin
James Iliff	William Rapp

Holland, N. J., Oct 18, 1892

From: The Milford Leader,   Whole No. 669
Thursday, January 5, 1893

Early Settlers of Holland Twp. Continued

Sometime prior to the Revolution, perhaps several years, Jacob Vanderbelt settled on 250 acres of land adjoining Phillip Bellis, and like most of the early settlers on the mountain was first a renter and afterward bought it of James Parker. Jacob Vanderbelt was a blacksmith by trade. In 1802 he conveyed 103 acres of his land to Jacob Stull. In the survey thereof its Eastern line ran between Vanderbelt's house and shop which he had previously erected near the middle of his tract and which compelled him to erect other buildings on the Eastern side of his remaining land (This circumstance explains whose shop it was that had been erected on the Capt. Hart farm at some early date, of which mention was made in a former letter). Who Jacob Vanderbelt's ancestors were we do not know, nor where he came from. He appears to have been married and had children as follows: William who married Mary Bellis, (they were married Feb. 27, 1817), John, Susan, who married Ralph Robbins, Rachel married to Ephraim T. Dalton, Fanny who married Jacob Bloom and Mary who died unmarried. He may have had other children we don't recall. Jacob Vanderbelt was succeeded by his son William who lived on and worked the place until his death about fifty years ago. After his death his widow held the farm until the majority of his youngest child, after which it was sold to Solomon Wieder who sold it to Wm. Phillips, the present owner. William and Mary (Bellis) Vanderbelt's children were: Peter, Herbert, Jacob, John, Duillious, William D., Firman and Elizabeth. Sometime before 1813 Jacob Stull, who had bought 103 acres of Jacob Vanderbelt died. After Stull's death his land appears to have fallen into the hands of Herbert and Phillip Bellis. In 1821 by virtue of three judgements obtained against the said Herbert and Phillip Bellis, by Thomas Stewart, Elsey Stull and Phebe Vanderbelt, respectively, this Stull land was set up at Sheriff sale and sold to Elsey Stull for $150 subject to all prior liens. After the decease of Elsie Stull her two sons Jacob and Henry had the place for about two years when Henry died, leaving Jacob sole owner until 1829, when he sold it to Daniel Hart who held it until his death which occurred in 1860. Daniel Hart was the son of John and Elizabeth (Roup) Hart and was born February 22d, 1790. When Daniel was about five years old his father died, leaving him and a younger brother (Peter) dependent upon his mother, who not having means to support them gave Peter to her brother, Peter Roup, and bound out Daniel to Aaron Sutton, of Fox Hill, this county. Daniel at this time was about six years old. Here he remained until he was eighteen years old when Sutton threw a stone at him and threatened to kill him. He then concluded to run away and hunt up his mother whom he had not seen for twelve years, and accordingly gathered together as much of his clothing as he could tie in a handkerchief and with what he had on his back started out early next morning and in the evening reached his uncle Peter Roup's then living on this Stull place. Here he found his brother Peter, and also learned that his mother had married Daniel Hawk and was then living on one the Durham Furnace farms in Durham, Pa. The next day accompanied by his brother Peter he went over to Durham to look her up. Having found her and spending a few days with her, he indentured himself for three years to John Riley then living in Durham to learn the blacksmith trade. Some time after this Aaron Sutton having learned of his whereabouts had him arrested and held as a runaway; but having shown that his master threw a stone at him and threatened to kill him, the Court decided that he need not go back again. At the end of his term of apprenticeship he had the trade and money enough to get married, buy himself a bellows and anvil, and the permission of Mr. Riley to use his shop and tools to make himself a pair of tongs and hammer, and with his wife and stock in hand started for New Jersey. Crossing the river at Johnson's Ferry he gave the last fifty cents he had to Hart Johnson for rum to treat the movers on, and thence moved into the house and shop near the old log school house in Holland, John Sinclair learning of his penniless condition handed him five dollars, bade him get some iron and go to work. Here he lived about five years and then bought himself twelve acres of land of what is now Amsterdam, built on it a house and shop, where he remained until 1829, and then bought the Stull place and carried on farming and blacksmithing here until his death. As before stated, Daniel Hart was the son of John and Elizabeth (Roup) Hart, born Feb. 22, 1790, and was married to Nancy, daughter of Nathaniel and Lorana (Taylor) Thatcher, who was born June 15, 1786, and died June 15, 1875, Their children are Thatcher who married Harriet Bellis, David who married for his first wife Rebecca Wetherel; his second wife's name we don't know; he is the father of twenty-one children. Peter married Ann Britton, Eliza married Herbert Sinclair, Lorana who married John Moore, and Aaron who died young. Their son Peter was mustered into the United States service of the late war as Captain of Co. F, Thirty-first Reg. New Jersey Vol., at Flemington, June 2d, 1862.

Jesse Sinclair

Dec. 29, 1892

For Sale-

A house and lot containing 7 acres all planted with fruit of all kinds situated near Holland school house, known as the "Hillside Hennery." Any reasonable offer will be accepted. Address A. Rapp, Bureau, Bureau Co. Illinois

---

For sale—three good work horses. One a bay mare 4 years old: one mare 7 years old, a good roadster; also one small pony. Call on or address Stewart Opdycke Little York, N. J.

Early Settlers of Holland Twp. Continued

Lying on the South of the Vanderbelt and Hart land was a tract of several hundred acres of land designated as being a part of Parker's land in Hunterdon county, and distinguished in a map of division thereof as Lot No. 14, a part of which, consisting of about 200 acres, Henry Metler and James Davis seem to have early seized and held, for a time, as tenants in common. In 1798 they made a division thereof and Henry Mettler and Elizabeth, his wife executed to James Davis a partition deed for 88 acres as his share of said land; and at the same time James Davis and Mary his wife, made a like deed to Henry Mettler for his share thereof. In 1803 James Davis conveyed his eighty-eight acres to John Sinclair, and probably at or near the same time Henry Metler conveyed his part to Michael Fackenthall, of Durham, Bucks county, Pa. Whether Michael Fackenthall ever lived on this land we do not know, but are inclined to think he did not, as he was at this time a large land owner in Durham. In a map of division of John Sinclair's lands made in 1818 we find Fackenthall mentioned as being still the owner of this land: but it could not have been long after this time that he sold it to Ralph Robbins. The traditions say that when Fackenthall sold this farm to Robbins he reserved thereout and donated to the public about one acre on which to build a church. It is perhaps worthy of mention here, to say that if Mr. Fackenthall could visit this place today; he would find things here fixed just as he left them eighty years ago. The church has never been built, nor has the land donated been enclosed, or used for any other purpose—than as then—a way to travel up on the Musconetcong Mountain. We think that Mr. Fackenthall must have been a good old man; no wonder he got rich. He is said to have been an only son of Phillip Fackenthall who emigrated to this country in 1784. Michael Fackenthall lived in Durham and owned large tracts of land.

Ralph Robbins having bought this land, and being an industrious and frugal man, afterwards acquired considerable other property, and at the time of his death was considered to have done well. Of the parentage of Mr. Robbins we can not recall having ever known anything. He married Susan Vanderbelt by whom he had children— Abigail, Jacob, Jane and Wesley. Abigail Robbins was married to George Eichlin and had children—John R., Caroline and Ralph. Jacob Robbins was married to Sarah Ann Starnar, had no children. Jane died unmarried, and Wesley who with Hummer Bellis, was killed by lightning while at school in Holland, sixty years ago.

As before stated James Davis sold his eighty-eight acres to John Sinclair in 1803. In a map of John Sinclair's lands made in 1813, we find five acres set off this tract and designated as Lot No. 1, (now Catharine Vanderbelt lot) and the remaining eighty-three acres designated as Lot No. 2, and is now lands of John Ulmer and James Eichlin. By the will of John Sinclair dated May 8th, 1817, and probated Sept. 14th, 1821, Lot No. 2 was devised to his son William Sinclair subject to a payment of eight hundred dollars. William Sinclair was a stone mason by trade which business he carried on with his farming, more or less, until his death. Meanwhile he acquired an additional house and lot of twelve acres adjoining his first land; also about twenty-four acres adjoining Alban White, John Cooley and others, and ten acres on "Gravel Hill" adjoining lands of Nathaniel Britton, Michael Fraley and others. In 1838 William Sinclair died, leaving his will dated June 9th, 1838, and proved August 7th of the same year, by which will he devised fifty acres of this northwestern part of his eighty-three acre tract to his son John H. Sinclair, and the remainder thereof, together with the adjoining twelve acres and the ten acres on "Gravel

Hill" to his son George W. Sinclair; and the twenty-four acres adjoining Alban White and John Cooley, together with one thousand dollars, to his son William Sinclair, who was also a stone mason; and eight hundred dollars to his grandson, Holaway Grandlee. William Sinclair was the second son of John Sinclair, and was born Sept. 25th, 1786, and was married to Mary Zearfoss, and had children; John H. Sinclair who married Mary Bloom and had children Robert, Amy Jane, Matilda, Cyrus, Belle Laurie, Maggie, George, William, Holaway, and Geo. W. Sinclair who married Mary Snider, and had one child William; William Sinclair who married Margaret Trauger and afterwards moved to Ohio and had several children; and Sarah Ann Sinclair who married William Grandlee and had one son, Holaway. About fifty years ago John H. Sinclair and Peter Snyder kept a store at this place, but not being much of a financial success, was after a few years abandoned. About seventy-five years ago Daniel Hart built the first blacksmith shop here, which was continued and successfully worked for many years. Today a blacksmith here would starve to death; and he would not be long in doing it, either.

Jesse Sinclair

Jan. 5, 1893

**From: The Milford Leader,   Whole No. 671
Thursday, January 19, 1893**

Early Settlers of Holland Twp. Continued

Another part of Parker's land, Lot No. 14, and adjoining the part last mentioned, was about sixty acres long known as Burgstresser's land. In the partition deeds between Metler and Davis executed in 1793, this land is mentioned as John Penwell's land. Whether Penwell ever lived on it is not known. He is supposed to have been a brother of William Penwell, who appears about this time to have been the owner of considerable lands in Nockamixon township, Pa., among which was the celebrated "Ringing Rocks" land, which he afterwards conveyed to Tunis Cox, of Philadelphia, and which was purchased by Tunis Lippencott in 1840.

Sometime prior in 1813 Phillip Burgstresser
bought of Penwell this land in Holland; and being a tanner
by trade, he soon after established a tannery here and
carried on the business of leather making until his death,
in 1841. He also built a nice brick house and good barn
and put other improvements on his place which were quite
superior to that of his neighbors at that period. Phillip
Burgstresser was probably a son of John Burgstresser
who lived in Tinicum township in 1812, and served in the
Revolution war. He was quite an influential man in
Holland in his day, and was one with Jacob Snider, John
Eichlin and Michael Fraley to whom John Sinclair in 1817
conveyed eighteen hundred square feet of land, in trust,
on which to build the Holland eight-square school house.
The first school at this place was built of logs and stood
about fifty yards East of the present one. He was always
called squire Burgstresser, but I do not think he was ever
a Justice of the Peace. He had the largest collection of
books of anyone in this community. At the sale of his
personal effects the writer bought his book case. It is
about 80 inches high and 20 inches wide; he had it nearly
full of books. Phillip Burgstresser, was born April 1st,
1778, and was twice married. His first wife's name I
cannot recall. They had one son Wilson, who married
Salome Eichlin, and had children, John, George, Maria,
Sallie. His second wife was Mary Dimmick, who was born
Jan. 5th, 1789, and died June 14, 1857. Their children
were Gustavus, Samuel, Elcana, Nancy, Phillip, and
Joseph D. Gustavus married Sallie Walters and moved
from Holland many years ago. Samuel is married to Jane
Dalton and have one child, Stewart. Elcana and Nancy
died unmarried. Phillip married ......Pursel, and moved to
Ohio. Joseph D. Burgstresser married Diana Pursel, and
have two children, Eli P., and Walter.

Moving Westward from Burgstresser's we soon
come to a quiet little hamlet called Amsterdam. Among the
early settlers at this place was James Smith, who about
1794 purchased fifty acres of land in and around the
village, and built the first and now oldest dwelling in
Amsterdam. James Smith owned this land until 1825, and
then conveyed it to Tunis Lippencott in consideration of
his keep for life. Mr. Smith was born about 1755 at
Derryghy, (Derr e a he) in the county of Antrim, Ireland,
and about 1780 sailed from Donegol for New York. He was

45

a weaver by trade, but for some reason he first sought and obtained employment at Andover, Sussex county, N. J., Iron Works. But these works having been confiscated and sold for the benefit of the Government, were at the close of the Revolution abandoned for want of timber for fuel. He next found employment for a time at Oxford Furnace,. after which he came to Hugh Hughes' Forge, but did not obtain work at that place. He next went to Durham where he found work, and where he appears to have been employed for several years after he bought the above named land. James Smith probably married soon after coming to America. His children were John, James, Thomas, Nancy, Mary, Martha. John married Rachel, daughter of Nathaniel Thatcher. Nancy married Tunis Lippencott. Martha died unmarried. Mary married Wm. Thatcher; her children were Elizabeth, wife of Jacob Ulmer, and Sarah, wife of Jonas Rapp. Thomas was married, and is remembered by the older people as the man who many years ago kept tavern on Northhampton St., Easton, Pa., and weighed 600 pounds.

Tunis LIppencott having become seized of Smith's land as before stated, lived on and farmed it until 1839 when he sold it in lots to Samuel Sinclair, John Kooker, John H. Sinclair, and George W. Sinclair. In the Spring of 1840 Mr. Lippencott moved to the Ringing Rocks farm in Nockamixon, Pa, where he resided until within a few years of his death, two or three years ago. Tunis Lippencott and Nancy his wife were parents of the following children: Martin, Lewis, John, James, William, Jane, and others I cannot name with certainty. Since writing the above there came a tradition to me that Phillip H. Rapp was the first purchaser of the Smith land as well as that of Elias M. Rapp adjoining it, and that Phillip H. Rapp owned all the land from this point to the Delaware River. However, should the tradition prove true, it will not materially affect what has been written.

Jesse Sinclair

Jan. 12, 1893.

From: The Milford Leader,   Whole No. 672
Thursday, Jan 26, 1893

Early Settlers of Holland Twp. Continued

The first settler at the point on the Musconetcong mountain called Sinclair Hill and who is the progenitor of the families still dwelling there by that name was Peter Cincleare, who was born in Germany in 1719, and emigrated to America in 1753, bringing with him his wife, Elizabeth and three children, John, Peter and Elizabeth. After a tedious voyage of eleven weeks he landed in New York, and from thence with his family started out to find a place and a home with good spring water and out of the way of beggars. He found that place exactly at the point on the mountain above mentioned, and there halted, and formed a tenantcy with Sir Robert Barker, of Bushbridge, Great Britain which was continued until his death in 1784, a period of 31 years. His wife Elizabeth was born in 1724 and died in 1798 So far as known they had no other children than the three which they brought with them from Germany. They are buried in St. James Lutheren Church graveyard at Greenwich, N.J. near its gate of entrance, and among the earliest buried there.

As a matter of interest we mention an incident that occurred about 1760, as follows: early one morning about that period, Richard Arnold, then living somewhere along the Musconetcong Creek, near its mouth, shouldered his gun and started over the hill for Holland. When he reached the top of the hill he saw in the twilight of the morning an animal resting on the limb of a tree on which he thought best to level his old flintlock and bring it to the ground. It was a panther. A light snow having fallen during the night, he took the animal's tracks, which led him to Peter Cincleare's log stable, where it had been during the night and killed a calf.

After the death of Peter Cincleare, his son John, who had always lived at home and was married, continued to farm under lease the same land upon which his father had first settled until 1793, when he entered into a contract with John Cooley, agent for James Parker for 128 acres of land which was subsequently conveyed to him by the said James Parker, and was the homestead on which he lived until his death. This tract is still in the names of his descendants. In 1799 John Sinclair bought of James Benson 4 acres (now Aaron Rapp's lot). In 1803 he bought of James Davis 88 acres (now John Ulmer's and James Eichlin's), and in 1813 purchased of Jacob Sailor 12 1/4 acres (now Thatcher's land). In about 1799 the homestead house was destroyed by fire, and afterward replaced by the one in which Simeon D. Sinclair now lives. John Sinclair was born in Germany Nov. 12, 1743, and died Sept. 1, 1821. He married Ann Albach (Alpaugh) who was born in 1761, and died (date lost). They are also buried in St. James Churchyard. John Sinclair and Ann (Albach) Sinclair had nine children: Peter b. Dec 5, 1784, William b. Sept. 25, 1786, John b. Jan. 2, 1789, Reuben b. Sept. 3, 1790, Samuel b. Dec. 28, 1791, Elizabeth b. Sept. 27, 1794, Ann b. Mar. 9, 1796, Mary b. June 2, 1799, Jesse b. Sept. 16, 1802. Peter Sinclair was trice married. His first wife was Ellen Craig, by whom he had children, John, Benjamin and Sarah. His second wife was Martha Snyder, children, Jacob, Peter and Mary Ann. His third wife was Ellen Thatcher, one child-Hart. William Sinclair married Mary Zearfoss, children-John H., George W., William and Sarah Ann. John Sinclair married Charetta Smith, children-William, Herbert, John, James, Eli, Andrew, George, Ann Marie, Margaret, Eliza, Marenda, Lucinda and Caroline. Rueben Sinclair married Ann Moore. Their children were Ann, Levi, Elenora, Abigail, Elizabeth, Aaron and John W. Samuel Sinclair married Permelia VanCamp, had children-Jesse, Peter, Letitia, Ann and John V. Elizabeth Sinclair was twice married, her first husband was Henry Snyder, had children-Peter and Mary Ann. Her second husband was Jasper Royce, children- Amy, Sophia and Lucinda. Ann Sinclair was married to Andrew Sailer, children-Daniel, John and Margaret. Mary Sinclair died unmarried. Jesse Sinclair married Susan Taylor (her maiden name was Sailor). They had no children.

As for Peter Cincleare's other two children, Peter married Mary Snyder. She was the child of Henry Schneider and was born in Holland Nov. 27, 1757 and came to America in 1766, had children-John, Peter, Hugh, Elizabeth, Lorana, Amy, perhaps others. [Editor's Note: A correction seems necessary here. In the will of Mary Snyder Sinclair Hice found in the Hunterdon County Surrogate's Office, written June 11, 1834, probated 1841, she lists the following as her children by her first husband, Peter Sinclair: John Sinclair, Elizabeth Werts, wife of Peter Werts and Peter Sinclair. As her son Peter was deceased she then listed his children – Hugh, Mary, Uri, Larani, and Amy.] Amy married Jacob Haughawont and was mother of Peter Haughawont, late of Holland. Elizabeth married John Mettler, who was early settled on the now Hummer farm, half a mile East of Milford, on the road to Mt. Pleasant. They had children among whom were John, Levi, Benjamin and others. John married Elizabeth Kels. Their children-Mary, Salome, Ann, Hiram, Sylvester, Amanda, Lucretia, Catherine and Margaret. Levi married Margaret Case, children-Abbey, Mary Ann, Jane, Margaret, Emeline, William, John and Lewis. Benjamin married (?), children-Levi, Christina, Alva and others. Levi married Marshee Kugler and had one daughter, Elizabeth, who is the wife of the honorable Wm. A. Martin of Frenchtown, N.J.

Jesse Sinclair

Jan. 19, 1893

From The Milford Leader   Whole No. 673
Thursday February 2, 1893

Early Settlers of Holland Twp. Continued

The ancestors of the Sniders', at one time quite numerous in this section, and many of whose descendents are still among us was one Henry Schneider who emigrated from Holland to America in 1766, and first settled near Newtown, Bucks county, Pa., he having been persuaded to emigrate and settle there by the Slacks and Vanhornes who had previously came from his neighborhood in Holland to that place. It does not appear, however, that he remained at Newtown longer than one, or two years at most, when he started out in search of a home elsewhere. Just how or why he chanced to come into Holland, N. J., is not known. There was a tradition that he stopped over night with Peter Cincleare, that they sat up and talked all night; and having kindred social qualities, dispositions and tastes, took to each other and were friends; and when the morning came, Henry Schneider chose for his home about 200 acres of unoccupied land adjoining Mr. Cincleare on which he moved, and the two lived side by side and were fast friends from the time they first met and talked all night, until death parted them in 1784. Whether Henry Schneider ever owned this land or was only a renter, I have no evidence. The first reliable evidence as to the ownership of it, shows that sometime prior to 1790 that tract had been divided into three parts and was owned by Schneider's sons, Martin, Jacob and Leonard; and that prior to 1813 Leonard died and Martin moved West and Jacob was the owner of the whole, or nearly so, until his death in 1837. Henry Schneider was the father of eleven children, Mary, born Nov. 27, 1757; Henry, born June 11, 1759; Jacob, born April 2, 1762; John, born Sept. 20, 1763; Catharine, born Dec. 28, 1765; Suzanna, born April 11, 1768, Martin, born Aug. 23, 1771; Leonard, born Aug. 20, 1773; Elizabeth, born Aug. 21, 1775; George, born March 18, 1777; Frederic+, born March 23, 1782.

Mary Snider, first born of Henry Schneider, was twice married. Her first husband was Peter Sinclair who was born in Germany about 1745, by whom she had children, John, Peter, Hugh, Elizabeth, Lorana, Amy,- perhaps others. Her second husband was John Hice. [Editor's Note: A correction seems necessary here. In the will of Mary Snyder Sinclair Hice found in the Hunterdon County Surrogate's Office, written June 11, 1834, probated 1841, she lists the following as her children by her first husband, Peter Sinclair: John Sinclair, Elizabeth Werts, wife of Peter Werts and Peter Sinclair. As her son Peter was deceased she then listed his children – Hugh, Mary, Uri, Larani, and Amy.] Henry Snider, second born of Schneider, at age seventeen entered the Continental Army and served under George Washington in all his campaigns. At the close of the war he married Mary Duzenberry and settled in Sussex (now Warren) county, on what is known as the Silver Hill farm, lying along the Musconetcong, about one mile above Hughesville. Among his children was Catharine who married Benjamin Opdycke and was the mother of nine children, and among whom was Albert Opdycke, late of Spring Mills, and a life long resident of Holland Township. Jacob Snider, third son of Henry Schneider, was a farmer, and married Mary Jones of Southampton, Bucks county, Pa. Mary Jones was a descendant of probably John Jones, whose name appears on Holmes map (1684) of Southampton, as the owner of land on the west side the old Street road; and was of Welsh descent. Jacob and Mary Jones Snider had also eleven children. Henry, born Oct. 24, 1789; Martha, born Aug. 18, 1791; Benjamin, born April 10, 1793; Jacob, born Jan. 25, 1795; John, born April 17, 1897; George, born March 30, 1799; Massey, born Aug. 7, 1801; William, born April 17, 1804; Lawrence, born June 11, 1806; Charles, born Jan. 18, 1811; Mary Ann, born Feb. 22, 1813. As for Jacob Snider's eleven children, Henry married Elizabeth Sinclair who was born Sept. 27, 1794; had children, Peter and Mary Ann. Martha married Peter Sinclair; had children, Jacob, MaryAnn, Peter. Benjamin married Rebecca Welch, born Aug 19, 1805; had children, Jane, Jacob, Peter, Sarah Ann, Elizabeth, Martha, Abby, Mary Catharine, Emma. Rebecca Snider is still living. Jacob married Ann Mettle, born July 10, 1803; children, Mary E., John M., Amy, Catharine, Martha, Margaret, Levi. John married Sarah Welch, born Dec. 28, 1803; children, George W., Catharine, Mary, John W., Abner, Mahlon, Henry, Lavina. George married Catharine Eichlin; children, John, Massey, Elizabeth. William married Sarah Melick; children, Mary C., Margaret, Hannah, Sarah, Electa. Massey died unmarried. Lawrence also died unmarried. Charles moved West and married Electa Austin, had children-names unknown, Mary Ann married Jacob Moore-no children. As to Henry Schneider's other children, John, fourth born, died soon after coming to America. Catharine, fifth born, married ----- Slack, a descendant of one of three brothers, probably Abraham, who came from Holland to Lower Makefield township, Bucks county, Pa., about 1744. Her children were Mercy, Mary, Catharine, Ann, Benjamin, Jacob. Suzanna, sixth born, became the first wife of Isaac Vanhorne, a son of Abraham Vanhorne, who emigrated from Holland to Northampton township, Bucks county, Pa., 1720. She died soon after marriage, and without children, so far as known. Martha, seventh born, moved West, of whom I know nothing. Leonard, eighth born, died comparatively young and is buried in Durham Cemetery. Elizabeth, ninth born, married Jacob Dewitt, a son of Jacob and Leah Dewitt, and a descendant of Andries and Tjerck Claus Dewitt, who settled in Ulster county, N. Y. c. 1648. Jacob and Elizabeth Dewitt lived and died in Wantage, Sussex county, N. J. Have no further knowledge of them. George, tenth born, married and settled at an early day on the late William Weller farm, Northwest of Hughesville. Had nine children, Henry, Mary, Suzanna, George W., Elizabeth, Abraham, Jacob, Thomas, Joseph. the later of these married Jane Butler, who also had nine children, of whom is George W., carriage maker and blacksmith, at Riegelsville, N. J. Frederic, eleventh born, was a tailor by trade and lived mostly in and around Finesville, was married and had children, Margaret, Matilda, Eliza, Lorenda, Mahala, Henry, William. Henry Schneider and Peter Cincleare are the only pioneer white settlers on land in this section, whose names are with any degree of certainty known to the writer.

Jesse Sinclair

Jan 26, 1893.

From: The Milford Leader,   **Whole No. 674**
Thursday, February 9, 1893

A Good Horse For Sale
I have decided to sell my horse. My reasons for selling him are as follows: (1st) He is eight years old. (2nd) He is perfectly sound and kind. (3rd) He will work wherever hitched. (4th) He is too fat and heavy for the road.
B. G. VanCleve, Milford, N. J.

For Sale - The undertaking business formerly carried on by L. R. Ulmer, deceased, will be sold at a bargain. Hearses and everything in good condition. Call on or address Wm. W. Ulmer, Administrator, Milford, N. J.

Early Settlers of Holland Twp. Continued

About 100 years ago Jacob Sailor settled on an oblong strip of land about ten to twelve chains wide, lying between lands of John Sinclair and Geo. Helms, and extending in length East and West from Jacob Vanderbelt's line to Thomas Purcell's land, and containing about sixty acres of land, on which Jacob Sailor erected for himself, first a log house, and afterward added to it a frame building, in and where he died an old man many years ago.
At some early period Jacob Sailor sold to one George Kresler about ten acres of the West end of his tract, on which said Kresler appears to have dug a well and built a

frame house. But some time before 1825 every thing pertaining to the house had been removed except the frame and an inside flight of steps and the place abandoned. Some years afterward Peter Fraley bought the premises and used the frame of the old house in part to build a carriage house.

Again, in 1813 Jacob Sailor sold to John Sinclair twelve acres off the Eastern end of his tract, and again in 1819 conveyed to Peter Sinclair about eight acres more from the same end of his place. Jacob Sailor was a jovial old Dutchman full of fun. I can remember him and his good old wife Margaret, as of yesterday; I am sure, of all the fine cake and pies I have since eaten, none have surpassed old grandmother Sailor's doughnuts and pies made from hog pumpkins and sweetened with molasses seventy years ago. I can taste them yet. Jacob Sailor was a farmer and of German descent. Of his ancestors we must not be too certain. There was a tradition and still is, that about the middle of the last century, two Sailor brothers, whose names were Jacob and Daniel, came into Northampton county, Pa.; that Jacob finally settled in Williams township, and Daniel went elsewhere and that Jacob Sailor had three sons, Peter, Jacob and Daniel-he probably had other children. Of these three sons, Peter, who was probably the elder one, remained in Williams township and was the original, or first Sailor pow wow doctor whose name and fame was extended throughout most of the European kingdoms and nations including that of his own. Jacob and Daniel came to New Jersey and settled in what is now Holland township; Daniel on a considerable tract comprising now land of Wm. Lippincott, Hart Sinclair, Jeremiah Clark in part, Maria Rapp and Wm. Rapp, and Jacob on the sixty acres above mentioned. Jacob Sailor was married to Margaret Roup (Raub). They had children, Andrew, Jacob, Suzanna, Rosana and Maria. His sons Andrew and Jacob first settled in Greenwich, Warren county, on what is since the Zeller and a part of Henry Super lands, and followed boating on the Delaware. One hundred years ago boating was an important occupation. The boats in use were called Durham boats. The first boat of the kind was built by one Robert Durham on the Delaware at the mouth of Durham Creek. They were built after the fashion of an Indian canoe, and were well adapted to navigation. They were

also of different capacity- the Sailor boys boats carried
225 barrels of flour-or twenty-four tons. Andrew Sailor
married Ann Sinclair, a daughter of John Sinclair and
granddaughter of Peter Cincleare, who emigrated from
Germany in 1753. Andrew and Ann Sailor had children,
Daniel, John, Margaret and Suzanna. Jacob Sailor was
married to Margaret Dickson, who was a daughter of
Thomas and Anna Dickson, natives of Durham, Bucks
county, Pa. Their children were Andrew, John, Samuel,
Margaret, Peter, Catharine, Phillip, Jacob, William and
Benjamin. Suzanna Sailor was trice married. Her first
husband was Taylor; her second Jesse Sinclair; and third
Alban White. She had no children by either husband.
Rosana Sailor married Phillip Bellis, and had children,
John, Jacob, William, Margaret, Lydia, Mary, Susan.
Maria Sailor was married to Skidmer Mettler, and had
children, William, Emma and Sarah. Jacob Sailor's
brother Daniel who was settled on the lands in Holland
now Wm. Lippincott's and others, above referred to, was
married and had children, Frederic, Abraham, Henry,
Catharine, Margaret, and three other daughters whose
names I do not remember. Frederic was married and had
children, but I never knew them. Abraham was a mute
and never married. After the death of his father, Henry
kept store for a while where William Lippincott now lives.
He afterwards married Sarah Lacey. Their children are
Mary and Jacob. Catharine Sailor was married to Isaac
Loar and had children, Joseph, Peter, Isaac, Catharine,
William, Elizabeth, Jacob, George. Margaret Sailor married
John Zellers, and had children, Peter, Samuel, Jacob,
Maria, Elizabeth and Ann. Of Daniel Sailor's other
daughters, one married a Mills, one a Raub, and the
other, Thomas Craig, (her name was probably Sidney). I
remember the names of some of their children which were
Samuel, Daniel, Henry and Sidney. Thomas Craig many
years ago moved to Michigan where several members of
the family soon after died. As to the family of Jacob
Sailor's brother Peter the doctor, I am not informed, except
that he had a son whose name was also Peter who
succeeded him as a doctor, and that Mr. Wilhelm, the
present pow wow, is said to have married a daughter of
the last Peter Sailor.

Jesse Sinclair

Feb. 2, 1893

Early Settlers of Holland Twp. Continued

Adjoining Henry Schneider was a tract of 125 acres called at an early day Moore's land. The first purchaser of this land was Christopher Roup; whether he was the first actual settler on it is not known. He bought it of James Parker In 1794. in 1798 Christopher Roup conveyed the tract to Andrew Roup, probably a brother. In 1800 Andrew Roup conveyed it to Frederic Trauger, and in 1806 Frederic Trauger sold it to John Moore, Innkeeper of Nockamixon township, Pa. In 1807 John Moore executed his will, in which he, among other things, did order and direct, that if all his children should be of lawful age, they, with their mother, Ann Moore, should be desirous of dividing his estate, and taking into their own hands their respective shares therein; then a partition be made as follows: Three shares to be allotted and given to the mother, Ann Moore, and the residue allotted, partitioned and divided equally among all his children and their heirs. This partition was made agreeably in the will in 1826. The partition deed says the will was proved at Newtown which shows that he must have died before May 1813, as the Bucks county office and records were at that time removed to Doylestown.

So far as known, John Moore never moved on this land, but I think he put a part of his children on it who worked it till his death, and after this his son John appears to have farmed it until its division in 1826. It was said that John Moore was a German by birth and that he wrote his name Mohr, but I have never seen it written in that way. In 1803 he himself wrote it the same as now, Moore. About 1776 he married Ann Kimball and kept a tavern in an old stone house which I believe is still standing near the riverbank between Milford bridge and Gwinner's place. He probably owned the house, though I have no certain evidence of it; but it is certain that he kept tavern in it until his death, and that he never moved to his farm In New Jersey. John and Ann (Kimball) Moore had eleven children, William, Christiana, John, Elizabeth, Jacob, Nancy, Archibald, Lavina. Catharine, Thomas R.

and Abigail. William Moore first purchased of Thomas Purcell the two lots owned by Andrew Lippincott and William Eates. He married for his first wife ———— Cooly, by whom he had John, who married Ellen Dillon, the mother of Daniel F. Moore and Anna Moore; Christiana, who married Michael Fraley and had William, Catharine Ann, and Oscar; and Nancy who was the second wife of John Dillon and had children Ellen, Christiana, Cornelia, William, Mary, Emma, Frank and Nathan. William Moore's second wife was Lydia Lippincott. Their children were Johnson, Wm. L., Sarah, Elizabeth, Mary and Hannah. Christiana Moore born in 1781 was married to John Williams who was born in 1780, and was the eldest son of Jeremiah, and grandson of Benjamin Williams, who came from Wales to this country as early at least, as 1750. John and Christiana William's children were Mary, Newberry, Ann Eliza, Barzilla, James, and Caroline. John Moore was a farmer, and after leaving his father's farm on which he lived from the time of, or perhaps before, his father's death, until its partition in 1826, moved on the now Capt. Hart farm, where he remained for two years when it was sold; whence he moved to the old Michael Zearfoss place at Durham where he continued for a time and then sold out and quit the business. John Moore married Elizabeth Harris and had children Jacob, Mary, Thomas, Daniel, John, Elizabeth, Wilson, Ann, Caroline, Newberry and William. Elizabeth Moore born in 1786, was married to James Iliff who was a descendant of one Richard Iliff who came from England and settled in Kingwood, New Jersey, prior to the Revolution. This Richard Iliff had a son John who married a Miss Williams and settled in Tinicum, Pa. Among their children was James, born in 1786, and who was married to Elizabeth Moore Feb. 14, 1807, and had children Jane, William, Margaret, Richard, John, Benjamin, Mary, James and Joseph.

James Iliff was one of the Presidential Electors to the convention that placed Wm. H. Harrison in nomination for the Presidency in 1840. Jacob Moore was twice married, first to Sarah Lippencott; his second wife was Mary Ann Snyder, had no children. Nancy Moore born in 1795, married Reuben Sinclair, born in 1790, and a son of John, and grandson of Peter Cincleare, who came from Germany in 1753. Reuben and Nancy Sinclair's children were Ann, Levi, Eleanor, Abigail, Elizabeth, Aaron and John W. Archibald Moore married Mary, daughter of Nathaniel and Lorana Thatcher. They had no children. Lavina Moore married Wm. Goddard. They had a son Edmund and I think one George and Rachel-perhaps others. Catharine Moore was married to John Purcel and had children John, Brice, Daniel, Hannah, and one whose name I don't recall, may have been more. Thomas R. Moore married Sarah, daughter of Peter Sinclair, had children Archibald and Ann. Abigail Moore married James Clark, who was a native of England and emigrated to America about 1880. They had no children.

Jesse Sinclair

Feb. 9, 1893.

From: The Milford Leader   Whole No. 676
Thursday Feb. 23, 1893

Early Settlers of Holland Twp. Continued

About ninety yeas ago Jeremiah Clark settled on about 160 acres since known as Clark's land in Holland, the greater part of which is yet owned by his descendents. As to its first ownership I have no positive evidence. About forty years ago Abner Welch, then an old man, told the writer that one Joseph Loughley, (Lufflee)-1 think his name was Joseph-owned it before Clark; and that the little island and bar where Welch & Snyder's saw mill was built, were then called by the name of Loughley as well as the larger one now called Lynn's Island. This I think was correct, as may be shown by the fact that commissioners appointed by the States of Pennsylvania and New Jersey in 1786 to divide the islands and bars of the Delaware, called both these islands by the names of Loughley; and those are the names by which they are yet called in law. Permit me in this connection to say that in 1739 the large island was called Tinicum. It was so called in a patent granted by King George at that time to David Martin, of Phillipsburg, giving him the exclusive right of ferrying horses, cattle, etc., over the Delaware River at any and all points between Marble Mountain and Tinicum Island, a distance of thirteen miles, which is just about the distance yet between these two points. From what has been said above we learn that Loughley must have been settled here at a pretty early day.

Just when Jeremiah Clark bought this land I have no means of knowing but it was no doubt early in the present century. When he bought and settled here he appears to have come to stay; and accordingly soon after built the stone house in which Margaret Hager now lives, and was no doubt considered a fine house at that time.

About 1842 Jeremiah Clark divided his land into five parts and deeded it to his sons William, Richard, Enos, Josiah, and daughter Margaret, in consideration of certain annuities to be paid him during his life. All of his sons kept their lands, lived and died on them except Josiah, who sold his and made his home elsewhere. Jeremiah Clark died in the stone house above named in 1845-6. Where he came from or who his ancestors were I believe I never knew.

He was probably of English extraction as his name indicates. His wife, whose name I have forgotten, was I think, of Hollandish descent. Their children's names were William, Richard, Jeremiah, John, Enos, Josiah and Margaret – if any others I have forgotten them. William Clark was a sawyer by trade and worked many years on a mill on Loughley, now Lynn's Island. He was said to have been the first sawyer to use a hammer and anvil to spread the points of mill saw teeth before filing them, and it is quite a matter of interest, to the writer at least, to know and remember that it was he who sawed on Lynn's Island the lumber to build the house in which the writer was born in 1819.

William Clark married Margaret Smith, a daughter of Belteshazzer Smith, who was a German by birth and a tailor by trade, and was married to Susan Price who was a sister to my grandmother Vancamp, who lived in Nockamixon, Pa. William and Margaret Clark had children Smith, Sarah Ann, Mary, Susan, William, Louisa, Jeremiah, John and Amy. Richard Clark was a farmer all his life, and was married to Nancy Burk. She was a sister to Edward Burk who is still living in Holland. Richard and Nancy Clark's children were Johnathan, Levi, William, Robert, Mahlon, Ellen and at least one other whose name I cannot recall. Three of their sons, William, Robert and Mahlon, served in the late civil war. Jeremiah Clark died young and was buried in the old Joseph Godley grave yard on the river bank (now Peter Rapp land). John Clark when a young man became demented In mind and died single

58

and was buried at the same place with his brother Jeremiah. At the building of the B. D. R. R., in 1852 the workmen dug up the bones of somebody buried there; which were re-interred in another place.

Enos Clark was a blacksmith by trade which he followed for several years in Milford and Holland and then quit and went to droving, dealing principally in cattle and sheep. About forty-seven or eight years ago he planted the first peach orchard in this section. The trees bore heavily, but he could not sell a peach. The second year of its bearing he fitted up a small still, but that not paying him he cut the orchard down and never planted another. Enos Clark married Mary Hager, a daughter of Feltey Hager, who was the ancestor of all the Hagers in Holland. Their children were Margaret, Aaron, Sarah and Ann. Josiah Clark sold his farm to Peter Welch and moved away from Holland and afterward married Susan Morgan, and had one son. Margaret Clark was married to John Piatt. Their children were Clark, William, Mary and Sarah. They are all deceased except William.

Jesse Sinclair

Feb. 16, 1893

From: The Milford Leader   Whole No. 677
Thursday, March 2, 1893

Early Settlers of Holland Twp. Continued

Among the emigrants who came into Holland, chiefly from Tinicum and Nockamixon townships, Bucks county, Pa., about 1800, Daniel Sailor who came from Williams township, Northampton county, Pa., and settled on a tract of land next to Jeremiah Clark's land, containing about 200 acres and extending from the river Northward to Parker's "long line" as the same is yet called. This line was established by James Parker in 1793. It began in the Northwest corner of the Sailor tract in a line of Thomas Purcell's land and extended Eastward over Gravel Hill into the line of the Hamilton tract. All of the line West of Gravel Hill remains the same as Parker made it. John Cooly, who was Parker's agent to sell his land in Holland, and who, in consideration for his services therefor, was allowed to select 300 acres from any part of Parker's land he might choose, located the same East of

Gravel Hill on both sides of this line and thus obliterated it at that point. The immutability of this line is proof of the unchanged condition of the lands of Holland that has existed for the past 100 years. Whether Daniel Sailor's land was a part of Joseph Loughley's tract I have not been able to determine. The little island and bar called Loughley, were a part of Sailor's land as already intimated. Sailor must have bought this land as early as 1800 if not before. One of the first things he done after the purchase of it was to build for himself the stone house which Wm. Lippincott now occupies, and which like his neighbor Clark's house, must have been a stylish one at that time. Whether Mr. Sailor ever engaged in any other business than farming is not known. He appears to have died not far from 1820. Upon his death his land was not sold, but either by his will or by commissioners appointed for the purpose, was partitioned and divided among his heirs at law. The stone house and 26 acres were set off to the use of the widow. The residue of his land lying South of the road leading from Milford to Johnson's Ferry was divided between his three sons, Frederic, Abraham and Henry; and the land North of said road was divided among his five daughters. Thomas Craig who had married one of the daughters, and therefor entitled to one share, bought up the shares of Mrs. Mills and Mrs. Raub, giving him three shares which he farmed for some years and then sold them to Frederic Ulmer and went West. Daniel Sailor's daughter Margaret, who married John Zellers and moved to Warren county, sold her share to Frederic Rapp; and Catharine, who married Isaac Lore, kept hers and lived on it until her death, a few years ago. Abraham who was a mute kept his and lived on it until he died. All the others sold theirs soon after obtaining possession of them. After the death of the widow about 1838 or 9 the house and lot set off to her use was sold to Andrew Sailor. About 1826 or 7 Abner Welch and Benjamin Snyder bought the share of Frederic Sailor and built thereon a saw mill which was run quite successfully until the big freshet in the Delaware in 1841. At that time the mill raised from off its foundation; but having been first well tied with strong ropes it swung toward the shore and was held, but the water wheel and most of the gearing and works, I believe was lost. The mill was again rebuilt and run until the next biggest Delaware freshet in June, 1862, when it was again

60

lifted from its foundation and carried away and was never built up again - lumbering on the Delaware having then ceased to be profitable. Some accounts of the families of Daniel Sailor and Benjamin Snyder having been given in former sketches, they need not be repeated here.

Of the ancestors of Abner Welch but little is known. The original Welch families are supposed to have come from Wales, and were Quakers. Abner Welch was born Oct. 15, 1774, and was the son of William Welch who was settled in one of the lower townships of Bucks county, (most probably Bensalem). Wm. Welch's children besides Abner were William, John, Joseph, Mahlon, Sarah, Martha, and Phoebe. John and Sarah - the latter married to a Wharton - moved to Luzerne county, Pa., while the rest of his family was settled in Hunterdon, Warren and Bucks counties, and are, I believe, the progenitors of all the Welchs in those counties. Abner Welch was married to Catharine Tinsman, who was born at Scott Mountain, Warren county, N. J., July 17, 1782. She was a daughter of Peter Tinsman then living at that place, but who afterward purchased the farm of late Henry Supers where he lived and died in the early part of the present century. After the marriage of Abner Welch he first moved on the farm of Isaac Shipman, in Greenwich, N. J., where he lived for several years, and next moved to the farm of Thomas Purcell, in Holland, where he remained until he moved to the saw mill about 1830. Abner and Catharine Welch had ten children: Sarah, born Dec. 28, 1803, and married to John Snyder; Rebecca, born Aug. 19, 1805, married to Benjamin Snyder; William, born March 5, 1807, married to Matilda Brink; Lenah, born Dec. 24, 1809, married to James Cooly; Christopher, born Dec. 9, 1811, married to Louisa Spouenberry; Peter, born May 22, 1814, married to Elizabeth Snyder; Martha, born June 18, 1817, married to Wm. Hunt; Joseph, born Aug. 2, 1820, married, first wife, Margaret Kooker, second wife, Mary E. Sinclair, whose maiden name was Snyder; Mary Welch, born Dec. 5, 1822, married to Peter Sinclair, and Catharine, born Sept. 14, 1826, who on the second day of Nov. 1848, was married to and became the first wife of Jesse Sinclair and was the mother of eight children, only two of whom are now living. She died November 15, 1870.

Jesse Sinclair

Feb. 23, 1893.

61

From: The Milford Leader   Whole No. 678
Thursday, March 9, 1893

Early Settlers of Holland Twp, Continued

Passing by for the present the settlement of
Parker's division of land in Holland, distinguished as lot
No. 26 we arrive at lot No. 27, usually known as Joseph
Godley land, the early ownership and settlement of which
I will now try to give some account. The tract contained
two hundred and eleven acres. I learn from an old
manuscript that the first person seized of this tract after
James Parker was one John Dawes. He probably bought it
of Parker. Sometimes after his seizure thereof John Dawes
conveyed it to William L. Potts, of Nockamixon, Bucks
county, Pa., and John Hughes of Montgomery county, Pa.,
as tenants in common. In 1809 John Hughes conveyed
one undivided moiety thereof to Francis Wade, of the city
of Baltimore, Md, merchant. On the 21st day of April,
1810, the said Francis Wade and William L. Potts, as
tenants in common, conveyed the said lot No. 27 to
Joseph Godley, of Alexandria, Hunterdon county, N. J., for
the consideration of $5584. Soon after Godley's purchase
of the tract he built a saw mill on it. He located his mill at
the creek; that location being about 30 rods above the site
of the present mill. It stood where the culvert now is
through which the creek passes across the B. D. R.R.
Were that mill now standing, all passengers and freight
carried over this road would pass directly through it. Mr.
Godley may have been wise in many things but he never
thought of the railroad running through his mill. Tradition
says that Mr. Godley was counted shrewd in business;
that he acted wisely in building a mill. It brought to him
much gain and by it he prospered well for a time. But one
day he thought that if he only had his own timber land
and get out his own timber and raft and run them down to
his mill he would make money faster. Acting along the line
of these thoughts he purchased a large tract of pine and
hemlock timber at some point on the upper Delaware,
where he placed men and teams and set them to getting
out logs for his mill. But the men did not work very hard
in his absence and the logs cost him more than he could
buy them for; besides the purchase of the tract having

involved him in debt, the payment of interest, and other unexpected expenses and losses incurred from his timber speculation forced him to sell or allow to be sold of his Holland tract the mill and all land lying South of Milford road. The sale was made by the Sheriff sometime between probably 1816 and 1820. On his land lying North of Milford road he had a small house and where he lived and died in 1829 or 30 and is said to have been the first person buried in the Christian Church grave yard at Milford. His barn was struck by lightning and destroyed in 1828. Where Joseph Godley came from I never knew. He was a brother to Wm. Godley who lived at Spring Mills. He was married and had one son Mahlon. I can remember old Aunt Katy Mash, who lived in a small house about where Wilson Angel's house now stands, who I think was in some way related to Mr. Godley, but I cannot tell how. After the death of Joseph Godley his son Mahlon, who was his sole heir at law, in 1831 sold the land to Jacob B. Curtis and John Derr. And in the same year Jacob B. Curtis and John Derr sold it in lots to John Angel, George Hager, and Christopher Hager. Joseph Godley's mill and land South of Milford road and which was sold by the Sheriff, was purchased by Nathaniel Britton. After Mr. Britton bought it he built a new mill, locating his where the present mill now stands. He changed the location because of some defect of the dam of the former mill, on account of which it could not be made water tight. Mr. Britton's investment here turned out well. His mill did a good paying business and his land yielded large crops. He placed on his land good buildings and otherwise improved the property. He lived on it until his death in 1847. Upon the death of Nathaniel Britton his son, John C. Britton, bought the place. Not long after John C. bought it he died, also, after which the property was sold in lots to Henry Britton, Mrs. Wilson Angel and George Hager. Henry Britton afterward sold his to Peter Rapp. The mill is now used as a peach basket factory.

Figure 8. Peter Rapp's basket factory at Holland. Mr. Rapp is seen standing in the doorway. Photo courtesy of Richard LaFevre.

Figure 9. Peter Rapp's basket factory at Holland. Photo courtesy of Terry LaFevre.

Nathaniel Britton was married to Mary Carhart. Their children were John C. married to Sarah Quin, Eliza, married to William Krouse, another daughter married Frederic Krouse, Isaac G. married to Elizabeth Britton, Samuel married to Suzanna Zearfoss, Jane married to Samuel Tinsman, Ann married to Peter Hart, Nathaniel married to Rebecca McEntee, and David who died single. Adjoining Nathaniel Britton, where Wm. Fraley now lives, one Jacob Krouse was early settled and where lived and he died in 1827. After his death Samuel Cooly, William Housel and Michael Fraley, commissioners, sold his place to John Tomson in 1828. John Tomson built on it a nice brick house and then sold it to Michael Fraley. It was a part of Lot No. 26.

Jacob Krouse had eleven children, Frederic, Mary, Ann, John, William, Thomas, Jacob, Hannah E., Catharine, Suzanna and Samuel. Jacob Krouse, so long freight and baggage agent at the Milford depot, is one of above family.

Jesse Sinclair

March 2, 1893.

**From: The Milford Leader   Whole No. 679
Thursday March 16, 1893**

Early Settlers of Holland Twp. Continued

One day in England about 1800, two Angel brothers, whose names where John and Richard, were digging a ditch when a passer by said to them, "boys, why don't you go to America where you won't have to dig ditches?" It was a new thought to them which the more they pondered the more it commended itself to them as the proper thing to do; and accordingly not long thereafter and in accordance with the suggestion of the passer by sailed for America bringing their father with them which composed all the family at that time so far as known to the writer. They brought with them a whipsaw adapted to sawing out ship timbers-a business they had been engaged at in England and which they intended to pursue here. On landing probably at New York they shouldered the saw with a few other notions and one dollar in pocket, and started out to find a timber forest suitable for their business. They came across New Jersey in search of such a place but did not find it until they struck the Blue Mountain near the Water Gap. There they halted and began their first business operations in America. They remained there until the timber suitable for their business was exhausted-how long that was I don't remember-and then came to Gravel Hill; and thence to Nockamixon, Tinicum and Plumstead. The process gone through in the manufacture of a ship timber was to find a crooked tree, cut it down, hoist the stick on a high scaffold, mark out the size, one man get on the top, the other underneath it and run the saw vertically after the manner of a saw mill. The labor was little less than digging ditches but it paid better. After pursuing that business for eight or nine years they made a snug sum of money which they divided. Richard took his share and went to Western Pennsylvania, and thence to Athens Co., Ohio; and John gathered up his, married a Miss Brown, came into Holland, N. J., bought about 80 acres of land of probably Joseph Burson-Burson owned it in 1796-being a part of lot No. 28 on which he placed good buildings and otherwise improved the land, made money and added to it considerable other land.

About 40 years after the two brothers divided their ship timber monies and set up for themselves, they again came together and took account of stock, whereupon it was found that Richard owned twice as many acres in Ohio as John did in New Jersey; but John's land in New Jersey was worth twice as many dollars per acre as Richard's was in Ohio; and they said it was a tie. John Angel was a good citizen and an obliging neighbor. He was appointed the guardian of Elias M. and Margaret Rapp; was frequently elected to the office of school trustee and road supervisor-not great offices to be sure, and yet the best his neighbors had to give him and show the estimation in which he was held by them. He was a member of the Presbyterian Church and in politics first an old line Whig and then a Republican. John Angel and his wife Brown were the parents of Nelson Angel married to Margaret Ann Hager, and Sarah Ann Angel married to Charles Eates. John Angel's second wife was Margaret Calfe by whom he had Wilson, married to Hetty Fraley, John married to Sarah Ann Wieder and Hannah married to Newberry Lear.

Joseph Burson who previously owned John Angel's land had a brother whose name was James and who in 1794 became the owner of Parker's lot No. 19, a part of which being about 140 acres, he conveyed to one George Kresler in 1800, and which in 1809 the said Kresler sold to John Eichlin who was Kresler's brother-in-law. John Eichlin having bought it for a permanent home kept it as such until his death in about 1845 or 6. After the death of Mr. Eichlin it was sold to Ralph Robbins who soon thereafter conveyed it to his son Jacob Robbins, present owner. Whether John Eichlin placed on it the old farm buildings in which he lived I am not certain; he built the house near the school house for his son John who had then married. John Eichlin was an old fashioned Dutch farmer who always kept large, fat horses and drove a regular Conestoga team of which he was proud. He was a member of the Lutheran Church and a Democrat in politics. He came to Holland from Durham, Pa., where he had probably been born. He was married to Catharine Kresler whose profession was that of a midwife which calling she practised until she was no longer able to go from her home; and as in those days male physicians were rarely employed in her line of duties she naturally had an extensive practice and was quite successful in it. She was also a pow-wow doctor, which art she practised along with her other duties. She was considered a very useful woman in the community and the writer has often heard the old people wonder what they would do when old "Granny Eichlin" died.

John and Catharine Eichlin had children as follows: John Eichlin who was married to Catharine Fraley and had several children whose names I am unable to give correctly. George Eichlin married to Abigail Robbins and had children Ralph, John R., and Caroline. Samuel Eichlin married to Ruth Pursell whose children were Levi, Samuel, Archibald, James, Maria, Sarah Ann, Elizabeth, Hannah and Ruth. Charles Eichlin married to Sarah Ann Zearfoss and had children George, John S., Maria and Elizabeth. Catharine Eichlin married to George Snyder and had John, Mercy, and Elizabeth, and Salome Eichlin married to Wilson Burgstresser and had children Elizabeth, Maria, John, George and Sallie.

Jesse Sinclair

March 9, 1893

Early Settlers of Holland Twp. Continued

According to a tradition which appears to be
entitled to some credence, the progenitor of the Hagers in
Holland was one of two brothers who emigrated from The
Prussian Netherlands, a province of Germany, to America
about 1744. One of these whose name was Nicholas
settled in Morris Co., N. J., and the other, whose name is
unknown, settled in Bucks co., Pa., probably in
Bedminister and was the founder of Hagersville in that
township. Nicholas Hager who settled in Morris Co., had
two sons only, one of whom was a doctor; the other a
lawyer and are the ancestors of the strictly New Jersey
branch of Hagers. The wife of McEvers Forman was a
grand daughter of Nicholas Hager. The other brother who
settled In Pennsylvania it has been ascertained had at
least three sons whose names were John Feltey and Peter.
One of these, John, who was bom about 1748, married
Mary Troch and moved to Nochamixon where he lived
until 1800 and then moved into Holland, N. J., to the farm
of (now Jacob Robbins) and was a renter of it under
George Kresler for ten years. Sometime during the year
1809 John Hager contracted with Francis Wade, of the
city of Baltimore, Md., and Wm. L. Potts, of Nockamixon,
Pa., for the purchase of two lots of land; one of about
seventy acres, the other fifteen acres, the same being parts
of Parker lot No. 26 on which he had permission to enter
and build the house now owned by Francis M. Hager, and
to which he moved in the Spring of 1810, where he lived
twenty-eight days. and then while sitting in its back yard
fell from his chair and was dead. The building of the
house, his removal to it and his death, are supposed to
have occurred before the delivery of the deed-as to
reasonably inferred from old deeds which show that April
15, 1811, Wade & Potts conveyed the same lands and
premises to John Hager, Jun., of Nockamixon, who had
then probably performed in some manner his father's part
of the contract; and that in 1814 John Hager, Jun.
conveyed the same lands divided in two parts to George
Hager and Christopher Hager. It is supposed that during
the four years interval between the death of John Hager

and the latter conveyance his widow lived in the house and Thomas Craig farmed the land. The first house probably erected on this land was located on the Southwest side of it near Sailor's line and Wm. Rapp's land. There was also at this place a blacksmith shop, but who lived in the house or worked in the shop is not now known. In 1831 George Hager and Christopher Hager purchased of Jacob B. Curtis and John Derr about forty acres each adjoining their lands, besides two wood lots on Gravel Hill, the same being parts of formerly Joseph Godley's lands. When threshing machines came into use, probably in 1840. George Hager built a dam and water wheel with suitable gearings to run his machine by water power. About 1843 Christopher Hager constructed a dam and built a grist mill, which I believe is still in use and is owned by his son Francis M. Hager who is successor to his father's lands at this place. About the same year of 1843 George Hager enlarged his dam and water wheel and attached to it works and machinery adapted to chopping and grinding of feed-notably corn, cob and all, and was also adapted to grinding plaster. This mill is also in running order and is likewise owned by his sons George W. and Mahlon Hager who are also the successors to their father's lands and tenements In Holland.

About 1853 George Hager purchased of John C. Britton's estate about thirty acres formerly Joseph Godley's land South of Milford road, and Christopher Hager bought the house and lot (now Aaron Rapp's). John Hager, Sen., served for a time In the Revolutionary War. As already mentioned John Hager died suddenly to 1810, He had married Mary Troch by whom he had nine children, all of whom were born In Pennsylvania. Their names were Phillip, John, Peter, George, Christopher, Elizabeth, Mary, Maria and Jacob. Phillip Hager was married and had children John, Abraham, Ralph, Peter, who married Margaret Rapp, Susan, Mary, Elizabeth, married to Samuel Severs, Hannah married to Levi Zearfoss, and Sarah married to Lewes Segeaves. John Hager married Mary Trauger and had children Samuel, John, Levi, Christopher, Elizabeth, Catharine, Mary, Julian and Sarah. Peter Hager married Charlotte Zearfoss and had children Michael married to Sallie Taylor, John married to Elsie Bellis, William married to Elizabeth Fraley. Henry married to Sarah Hamlin, Margaret, Mary and Susan unmarried. George Hager married first to Salome Rapp had children Margaret Ann married to Nelson Angel, and Jacob married to Elizabeth Robbins; his second wife was Sarah Dimmick; children, Maria married to Jacob Rapp, George W. married to Amy Bloom, Mahlon, first wife, Margaret Snyder, second wife, Lizzie Pursel; Sarah married to Jacob V. Cooly and Lydia Ann married to Duillious Vanderbilt. Christopher Hager married Susan Dimmick and had children John D. married to Selenda Kooker; George A. married to Hannah Wright, Francis M. married to Catharine Ann Ulmer, Cornelius who is unmarried, David O. married to Eliza Vanderbilt, and Amy who died unmarried. Elizabeth Hager married John Starnar and had children Christopher married to —— Creveling, Elizabeth married Tunis Stires, Mary married to John Staats, Sarah Ann married to Jacob Robbins, Emma, first husband —— Blackwell, second, John K. Boileau, Julian married to Daniel Bloom, Charlotte married to Daniel Bodine and John who died unmarried. Mary Hager married Enos Clark and had children Margaret, married Elias M. Rapp, Aaron married to Mary Catherine Cyphers, Sarah married to John V. Sinclair, Ann married to William Davis and Andrew who died young. Maria Hager who died young and Jacob Hager who one morning on his way to school fell dead on land (now Tomson Fine's). His lifeless body was found in the afternoon of that day, by Michael Fackenthall, Esq., who chanced to pass that way. The writer Is indebted to Francis M. Hager for many facts narrated in the above sketch.

Jesse Sinclair

March 16, 1893

All kinds of paints and oils at S. Sinclair's hardware store.

**From: The Milford Leader   Whole No. 681
Thursday, March 30, 1893**

Early Settlers of Holland Twp. Continued

The Rapps living in Holland trace their origins to one Phillippus Henriccus Rapp who was a native of Zulz, Germany, a town of Prussian Selesia of 2700 people, 23 miles S. S. W. of Oppeln on the Biala in Upper Alsatia, where he was born, probably 1727 or 8 and emigrated to America about 1750 His father's name was Godfrey Rapp who was a Lutheran minister and preached in the town of Zulz. There is a tradition that he once visited America and preached for a time in the Lutheran Church at Germantown, Philadelphia, and then returned to Germany. His son Phillippus Henriccus Rapp upon his arrival to this country, settled in Nockamixon, Bucks county, Pa., where he afterward owned real estate, and was also a Lutheran minister and preached in Tohickon Lutheran Church from 1765 to 1769; and tradition further says that he also preached at Germantown. As already mentioned Phillippus Henriccus Rapp settled in Nockamixon and was the owner of land on which he lived and died; and is said to be buried in a private yard not far from where he first settled. He married a Mrs. Miller, widow of Godfrey Miller; her maiden name was Remley. She came from Germany to America with her mother and a younger brother when she was 14 years old. Her mother died on her way hither and was buried in the ocean. Miss Remley first married Godfrey Miller by whom she had one son whose name was John Frederic, who became a Lutheran minister and was the maternal grandfather of Elias M. Rapp and Margaret Hager. Phillippus Henriccus and wife Miller Rapp had 5 children. Phillip H., Cunard, Susan, Mary and one son name unknown. Mary married a Yost, and Susan a Roarbach; the latter went South. His son Phillip H. was born In Nockamixon in 1758, and at The age of 18 years joined the Continental Army and served in the Revolutionary War. At or near the close of the war he married Margaret Stein and remained in Nockamixon until 1801 or 2, and came in to Holland and bought 80 acres of Parker lot No. 28, on which a man by the name of Shannon was then living and of whom Mr. Rapp may have purchased. The place contained no timber, that having been cut off, either by the Indians who had been thickly settled there or some other unknown person. For several years Mr. Rapp brought his firewood from Nockamixon where he also owned land. The wood was sleded over the river in Winter on the ice. The timber for Frederic Rapp's barn it is said was brought from Pennsylvania. As the Rapps appear to have been either preachers, carpenters or undertakers, one of the first

71

things Phillip H. did on the place was to build himself a workshop. Upon the marriage of his son Frederic a house was built for him to live in. After Frederic Rapp vacated this house Phillip H. taught a free school in it. Daniel U. Sheets also kept school in it during the building of lower Holland school house. Sometime after Mr. Rapp's purchase of the 80 acre tract he bought 49 acres of Lot No. 19, now owned by Elias M. Rapp. This land had been previously owned by James Burson, who in 1796 sold it to Wm. Posten of whom Phillip H. Rapp probably bought it. After his son Joseph was married he moved to this place and built a house on it where Elias M. Rapp's house now is. There was on the place at that time an old house which stood a few rods East of the new one, which Joseph Rapp used for a workshop. That old house was used to hold bustling matches in. By the way, the writer one night, when half grown, attended a match in it and won a turkey. The next morning his father threatened to whip him for bringing a turkey on the place and his old grandmother pitched into him for gambling.

Phillip H. Rapp died in 1830 and was buried at Nockamixon. His funeral expenses were $7.00 paid H. Chamberlin for coffin and attendance, $3.62 ½ to Hart Johnson for ferrying funeral over the river, and $2.50 for Henry S. Miller for preaching the sermon. The appraisement of his personal property was $4890. After his death and upon the application of George Rapp and George Hager, Phillip Burgstresser, John Angel and Jacob B. Curtis were appointed commissioners to make a division of his real estate. They sold it Aug. 27. 1831 to Phillip Rapp and Frederic Rapp. It is supposed he had sold his Nockamixon land to his son George Rapp and his No. 19 place to his son Joseph or his widow during his lifetime. Phillip H. and Margaret Stein Rapp had children George, Jacob, Frederic, Joseph, Mary, Salome, Margaret, Augustus Peter, and Phillip. Margaret died when 14 years old and Augustus Peter at the age of 18 years. George Rapp, who is the great grandfather of Ryan Rapp, Editor of the Riegelsville News, married Mary Ulmer and had children, Francis, David, Isaac, Abraham, Lydia and Sarah Ann. Jacob Rapp married Susan Walters, had children, Henry, Catharine, Caroline, William, Phillip and Margaret. Frederic Rapp married Sarah Frankenfeld, their children were Catharine, Sarah Ann, John, Jacob, Lavina,

Margaret, William. Joseph Rapp married Dorothy Miller, daughter of Rev. John Frederic Miller, and had children, Margaret and Elias M., Mary Rapp married John Ulmer, had children, Frederic, Margaret, Ann and Levi R. Salome Rapp married George Hager, had children, Margaret, Ann and Jacob. Phillip Rapp married Eleanor Ruth and had children, Jonas, Sarah, Eleanor, Joseph, Andrew, Peter, Margaret, Elizabeth and Cornelia. In 1813 John Ulmer bound his son John Frederic, then five years and three months old, and his daughter Margaret Ann, four years and two months old, unto Frederic Rapp until each should become fifteen years of age. John Tomson was guardian of Ann and Levi R. Ulmer, children of Mary Rapp, deceased; George Hager guardian of Margaret Ann and Jacob Hager, children of Salome Rapp, deceased, and John Angel guardian of Margaret and Elias M. Rapp, children of Joseph Rapp, deceased. In 1787 Phillip H. Rapp executed a power of attorney to John George Obermutter, of Germany, to collect a supposed fortune due him from his grandfather Godfrey Rapp's estate in Germany but the thing never "materialized" I am indebted to Jonas Rapp for many facts above narrated.

Jesse Sinclair

March 24, 1893

From: The Milford Leader   Whole No. 682 Thursday, April 6, 1893.

Early Settlers of Holland Twp Continued.

In 1797 Adam Shearrer, of Williams township, Northampton county, Pa., purchased 160 acres of Parker's land in Holland distinguished as Lot No. 29. Mr. Shearrer having bought it for speculation afterward sold it to Michael Freighley (Fraley) of Nockamixon, Bucks county, Pa., for 700 pounds. After Shearrer sold it he was offered more money and wanted to back out or down, but Mr. Fraley put down the 700 pounds Sterling in gold and silver coined money and held him to the contract, and in the Spring of 1800 moved to the place where he lived 48 years and then died.

The tract was the most Easterly and last of Parker's lands fronting the Delaware; its Southeast corner being also the corner to a line of division between Byerley and Parker(as that line is named in his deed).The tract was also the traditionary site of the Indian grasshopper war, and although the traditions had not then, nor have they yet been fully verified, yet Mr. Fraley was one of the many of 100 years ago who believed them well founded, the evidence whereof, then existing in that locality being ample enough to convince and satisfy the most incredulous. As among all of whom I have written that lived in Holland 100 years ago, none were great bankers, railroad kings, or millionaires; so neither was Mr. Fraley - only a farmer that was all, but then he was a good farmer; no dock, carrot, thistles, or other obnoxious weeds had any show on his farm. Besides enriching his land and growing large crops, he kept good buildings and fences on it. He also grew watermelons which he sold to the boys at the rate of six and a quarter cents for as many as a boy could eat at a time, though some boys he charged seven cents. Through the courtesy of his grandson, Wm. Fraley, there lies before me an old manuscript, from which I learn that some time during the minority of Michael Fraley his father died, and that Gertront Freighley, who is supposed to have been Michael's mother, was appointed his guardian and Michael Deamer her bondsman; and that when he was 18 years old he of his own free will and with the consent of his guardian indentured himself to Peter Mill, of Haycock township for two years and a half to learn the potters trade. The indenture executed May 7th, 1788, sets forth among other things that Michael shall serve his master faithfully, keep his secrets, not embezzle his goods, play cards, dice, or other unlawful games, not frequent taverns or ale houses, not get too intimate with the girls or contract marriage, etc., during the term aforesaid, and Mr. Mill to provide him with sufficient meat, drink, washing, mending, lodging, shoes, etc. But at the end of the term, Mr. Fraley having been a good apprentice, Mr. Mill thought to make him a present, and having nothing else handy by gave him his daughter Catharine, with which Mr. Fraley was well pleased and said "**Thanks**," Mr. Mill.

Who Michael Fraley's ancestors were I have not learned to a certainty. He was probably a son of Martin Freyley, who with several others, came from Germany to Tinicum, Bucks county, Pa., in 1702 and settled there as renters under Robert Stevenson, who then owned a large tract of land at that place. Michael Fraley was born April 16, 1770, and on June 28, 1793, was married to Catharine, a daughter of Peter Mill, she having been born November 23, 1772, by whom he had ten children, Peter, Michael, Jacob, Catharine, Elizabeth, Joseph, Sarah Ann, Charles, Abraham and Hettie. Peter married Mary Pittenger. After his marriage he bought a farm near Finesville where he lived until his death in 1874. He was a Republican in politics and a member of the Presbyterian Church. Peter and Mary Fraley had children, Margaret, Joseph, Helena, Elizabeth, Maria and Hettie. Michael married Christiana Moore and had children, Catharine Ann, William and Oscar. Mr. Fraley was a carpenter. After his marriage he first lived near Spring Mills until 1843, and then moved to the place where his son William now lives. He was a Republican in politics and a corporate trustee of Holland Presbyterian Church of which he was also a member. Jacob married Hettie Ruth and had children, William R. and Jacob - latter having lived many years in Easton, Pa., and is well known as a successful business man of that city. Catharine married John Eichlin and moved near Easton where they lived and died. Their farm is now a part of South Easton. Their children were Michael, Sarah, Henry, Charles, Catharine, Emma, Johanna, John and Joseph. Elizabeth married John Rockafellow, and had children, Eliza, Mary, Joseph, Sarah, Jennie, George, Alice, Hiram and Catharine. After their marriage they moved to Nunda, Livingston County, N. Y., and afterward to Crawford, Pa. where Elizabeth died; her husband afterward went from there to Nebraska. Joseph Fraley was twice married; his first wife was Johanna Rockafellow, his second, Mrs. Moulton. He had no children by either wife. Joseph's first wife was a sister to John Rockafellow and they moved to Nunda at the same time that John and Elizabeth Rockafellow did, where he died, both of his wives having died before he did. Sarah Ann married John Vansyckle who was a farmer and lived near Mount Pleasant. Their children were Mary C., David, Holaway, Hettie, Melinda, Margaret, Joseph, Samuel W., Lizzie and John E. Charles married for his first with Ann Lear and had one child, Joseph. His second wife was Margaret Hann, has one child, Ella. Charles' first wife died at Milford. He then went to Nunda, N. Y., where he married Miss Hann, came back to Milford for a time and

75

then returned to York State and is living at Mt. Morris, Livingston county, N. Y. Abraham died unmarried. Hettie married Wilson Angel and has one son, John W. Mr. Angel is a native of Holland and a farmer by occupation. He is a staunch Republican in politics, and an Elder in the Presbyterian Church at Milford of which he and his family are all members, (The last.)

Jesse Sinclair

March 30, 1893

▓ SKETCH OF HOLLAND PRIOR ▓
TO THE ORGANIZATION OF
THE PRESBYTERIAN CHURCH

From The Milford Leader   Whole No. 830
Thursday, February 20, 1896   (Part 1)

By Jesse Sinclair

Although the Holland Presbyterian Church is nearly half a century old, not a single record of its organization is extant. Some notes had been taken from the records of the Raritan Presbytery by Rev. Jonathan H. Sherwood for the purpose of writing its history but he died without doing it, and upon his decease the notes were lost, as were also at the same time the minutes of first four years' meetings of session: and presumably since then other matter relating to the church that would now be of interest has been lost, too. To remedy, in part at least, these losses and consequent defects, the writer proposes to give a sketch of Holland, her people and the religious movements and doings among them prior to and down to the period of the church's organization. *The Original Holland*, geographically considered, consisted only of the beautiful, fertile, little vale lying between the "Pennsylvania Narrows" or Delaware river, "Gravel Hill" and Musconetcong mountain, and was part of a large tract of land; the title to which, next to that of the Indians, was vested in the English Crown. Without noticing in detail the several conveyances of the lands of New Jersey commencing with the grant of Charles II to his brother James, Duke of York, in 1664 it may be here stated that the title of *West Jersey* having been vested in William Penn, Gawen Laurie, Nicholas Lucas and Edward Billings, these four persons on March 2nd, 1676, conveyed to Robert Squib one propriety of West Jersey, and in 1681, same grantors, another propriety, containing together 16,565 acres of land, which by the way constitutes nearly, what is now Holland township. On January 26, 1706, Squibs' executors conveyed the same to Thomas Byerley, who by his will dated May 26, 1725, devised one –half of said tract to Robert Barker, Esq., of England. The original Holland was a part of the Barker tract. Afterward Edward John Ball was seized of Barker's land, but when and how he came by it, I have not learned. On Jan. 4, 1793, Ball conveyed said land to James Parker, who in the same year employed Edward Welsted to survey the same into lots and farms. Whether the name *Holland* was derived from its low lands, or the early settlement of it by Dutch emigrants from "Old Holland," or both, is not known, but the latter seems the more probable. Edward Welsted mentions the place by that name in his survey of it in 1793. Prior to the white man's advent numerous Indians had long dwelt here. They belonged to one of the five tribes of the Delaware or Lenni Lenape nation known as the Wanamis. That tribe inhabited the southern half part of New Jersey. Holland constituted their northern limits, the Musconetcong Mountain being the dividing line between them and the Munsey tribe living north of that line. It is more than probable that there were two Indian villages or towns in Holland-one at or near the "Big Rock," the other on land formerly Jeremiah Clark's, (now Eli Heller's). Moses Tatamy, David Brainerd's Indian interpreter, is supposed to have been born at or near the lower village. And an old tradition asserts that the Indian Grasshopper Battle was fought here, but history fails to confirm the latter. They appear to have removed from Holland about the years 1742 to 1744.

[TO BE CONTINUED]

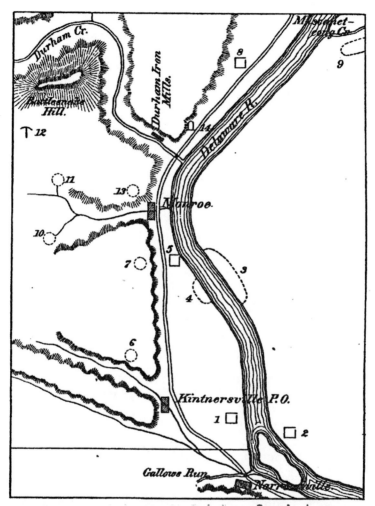

Figure 10. Map taken from The Annual Report of the
Smithsonian Institution for the year 1883 showing
Indian settlements in Bucks County Pa. and Holland N.
J.

[Editor's Note: Information for the above map taken from
the Annual Report of the Smithsonian Institution for the
year 1883: "No. 2 is also the site of an ancient village, on
the farm of Mr. Clark, one mile north of Holland Station,
Hunterdon County, New Jersey. The extent of this village

was not as great as that at No. 1, but it has added to our collection many fine specimens. Among these is half of the bowl of a stone pipe, the only fragment of a stone pipe yet found...Two stone axes of very rude workmanship were picked up at this place. The rudest is an ordinary cobblestone notched at the sides, near one end, and slightly grooved half way across one side. The other is an oval cobblestone, 11 inches in length, with a narrow groove around one end. No attempt seems to have been made to sharpen either of these axes.

No. 3 is a locality on the farm of Mr. Snyder, near Holland Church, where have been found a number of spear and arrow points, most of them broken. Tradition tells us that this was an ancient battle-ground. Two tribes lived in the vicinity, and the chidren, in their wanderings, met each other and quarreled about a large grasshopper which one of them found. This resulted in a war, and this localitiy is said to be the place where the decisive battle was fought. The conflict was witnessed by a white man from the opposite side of the river. Such is the tradition as it exists in the neighborhood.

No. 9 is on the farm of Mr. Riegel, near the mouth of the Musconetcong Creek, Hunterdon County, New Jersey. Spear and arrow points are found here.]

From The Milford Leader   Whole No. 831
Thursday, February 27, 1896   (Part 2)

Although Holland was an attractive spot settlements in it by the whites were slow. This was owing to the land composing it being held in an undivided state from the year 1664 down to 1793—as above indicated. This condition of the land tended to discourage settlements upon it, and although a few emigrants found there way here as early perhaps as 1750, as is inferred from their names afterward appearing as renters of Robert Barker in 1760, it was not wholly and permanently settled until after the partition in 1793. Between that period and the year 1800 most of the land was sold to purchasers who became permanent residents thereof. Nearly all the later settlers came in from Pennsylvania. The nationality of the people at that period may be classed somewhat as follows: The Burgstressers, Rapps, Hagers, Eichlins, Sinclairs, Sailers, Loars, Moores, and Blooms were of

German Ancestry; the Vanderbilts, Sniders, Mettlars, Welchs and probably Fraleys, of Dutch or Holland descent; the Clarks, Angells, Robbins, Tomsons, Godleys, Purcells, Lippincotts and Brittons of English extraction; the Craigs, Davis' and Smiths, Irish, and the Johnsons, Scotch or Welsh. I may have erred as to the lineage of some of these, but of most I think it correct. The state of religion among them appears to have been very low. The religious declension in this country at the close of the Revolutionary War—"Payne's Age of Reason" and other infidel writings sent to this country from France, and found in the homes of some of this people—had their baneful effects and produced a great declension of religions among them, so that with a few exceptions there was none. In probably the year 1832 an incident took place which is next mentioned, though not without some hesitation, it being as follows: One day a colporteur of the American Tract Society called at the school house and handed the teacher (Jacob B. Curtis) some religious tracts to be distributed among the pupils. For some reason the teacher thought best to have the consent of the parents before giving them out, and accordingly requested the children to ask for it. The next morning two of the parents appeared and forbade any distribution to be made, and during the same day the tracts were fastened to a pole about fifteen feet long, hoisted and planted near the school house, and in the evening many citizens of Holland came there to witness their burning, which was done amid cries of *down with priestcraft in this country.*

Whether there had ever been more than one or two sermons preached in Holland prior to 1825 cannot be determined; but all knowledge of it previous to that period seems to indicate there had not-though a period of seventy-five years had then elapsed since settlements were first made in it.

At some period between the years 1825 and 1830 Mrs. Abigail Roberts of the Christian persuasion commenced occasional preaching in Holland, which on account of its being something novel created a great religious awakening among this people, and gave rise to much animated—not to say angry discussion among them. However good came from it. It set the people to thinking. Most of the preaching in Holland at that period was done in an Octagonal, or as then called, "eight square" school house. During the decade 1830 to 1840 Rev. B. Chattell, Rev. George Banghart, and Rev. Jacob Hevener, Methodist ministers, from Warren and Sussex counties, N. J., preached each occasionally in Holland school house. Mr. Chattell was but seventeen years old and known as the boy preacher. Mr. Hevener was an itinerant and evangelist and called the "Old war horse" of Sussex county.

[TO BE CONTINUED]

From The Milford Leader   Whole No. 832
Thursday, March 5, 1896   (Part 3)

The first Presbyterian preaching in Holland of which the writer has any knowledge was about the year 1825 by Rev. Garner A. Hunt, a Presbyterian minister of the Presbytery of Newton. He usually preached in private houses though sometimes in the school house also. In 1833 he preached a dedicatory sermon of the house in which these lines are written. Mr. Hunt continued preaching in this neighborhood monthly for many years— indeed until the close of his long and somewhat eventful life, which terminated in 1849. Mr. Hunt being the pioneer Presbyterian preacher in Holland some further notice of him may be of interest. He was the son of Major General Augustine Hunt, an officer of the British army in the Revolutionary War. He married Ruth, daughter of Capt. David Page, of Cumberland county, N. J. He was first a Baptist minister and preached in said county. In 1796 he was called to the pastorate of Kingwood Baptist Church where he preached about ten years and then turned Presbyterian. In 1810 he was installed pastor of Harmony, Warren county Presbyterian Church by New Brunswick Presbytery. In 1818 his relations with Harmony ceased. In the same year he was called to Scott's Mountain Presbyterian Church, and in 1827 his relations to it also ceased. He owned a farm at Harmony where he lived and died, aged 84 years. Mr. Hunt first came to Holland to preach to Jacob Snider, a native of "Old Holland" who with his parents had settled here in 1766, he having been requested to preach here by Rev. Malichi Jones, a Welshman then preaching at Feasterville, Bucks county, Penna. Jacob Snider had married a Mary Jones, who was related to minister Jones.

82

A tradition in the Snider family says that Mr. Jones once preached to a few people in Mr. Snider's house while on a visit there, and was so far as known, the *first* sermon preached in Holland. There is also a tradition that the excentric Lorenzo Dow preached in Holland. The early church choristers of Holland were Benjamin Snider and Peter Sinclair. They were supplied with hymn books, but the minister usually lined the hymns for the accommodation of those who did not have books. They sang music written in the minor key only, the major key being then deemed to gay and sprightly for church use.

In 1837 Rev. John McNair preached in Holland, he being pastor of Milford and Kingwood Presbyterian Churches in that year. In 1838 Rev. Joseph Campbell, D.D. was installed pastor of Milford and Kingwood Churches. Mr. Campbell also preached in Holland once a month and had a bible class which he conducted semi-monthly. He continued preaching here until 1840 when he died. Dr. Campbell was of Scotch ancestry, thoroughly imbued with the principles and doctrines of the Presbyterian Church, was a good debater, an able preacher, prayed with his eyes open, and was doctorated by Lafayette College. He had formerly preached at Hackettstown, N. J. where his body was laid to rest. About this time spasmodic efforts to organize a Sunday-school in Holland began to be made. The first of the kind was a few sessions held by Daniel U. Sheets, a school teacher from Pennsylvania, in 1840. But with exception of singing their management and instruction was the same as the week day school. Between this period and 1847 several other attempts were made for this purpose by Miss Mary A. Snider, Miss Mary Williams, and Miss Eliza Brough, but without much success. In 1848 a Union School was organized with Jesse Sinclair Superintendent, and Isaac G. Britton Librarian; if there were any other officers I have forgotten them. The school was supplied with Sunday-school helps and literature as then existed and thereafter continued, except that it was closed for many years during the winter seasons. The first known convert brought to Christ through its instrumentality was Mary C., a eleven-year-old daughter of Benjamin and Rebecca Snider. She died about six months after its organization, testifying of it as the means by which she had been led to give her heart to the Saviour whom she

83

confidently expected to meet and be forever with in Heaven. The preaching and bible class instruction of Dr. Campbell no doubt had much to do with starting the Sunday-school movements above mentioned; and also materially advanced the Presbyterian cause in Holland. Dr. Campbell was succeeded by Rev. Jonathan H. Sherwood, called from Marksboro and Hardwick, Warren county Churches, to Milford and Kingwood in 1841.

[TO BE CONTINUED]

Figure 11. Jesse Sinclair home in which Rev. Hunt preached a dedicatory sermon. Photo courtesy of the Birkner family.

From The Milford Leader   Whole No. 833
Thursday, March 12, 1896   (Part 4)

Mr. Sherwood also continued Presbyterian preaching in Holland (but in Lower Holland School House the district then being in two parts). About one year and a half after coming here Mr. Sherwood was relieved of his Kingwood charge, and in lieu thereof was appointed stated supply of Red Hill Presbyterian Church in Bucks county, Pa., by the Presbytery of Rariton. Meanwhile he devoted considerable time to his Holland field with a view to organizing within it a Presbyterian Church at the earliest practicable time. In addition to his regular services he held a three days' meeting at Buttonwood Grove on John Bloom's bar at the Delaware River. He was assisted at this meeting by Rev. Jacob Kirkpatrick, D. D.,

84

Rev. P. O. Stoddiford, D. D., and Rev. —— Erwin, all of Rariton Presbytery; and Rev. George Junkin, D. D., L. L. D., of Newton Presbytery and President of Lafayette College. That river side meeting also advanced Presbyterianism somewhat in Holland.

There being at this time no churches in Riegelsville, and the Presbyterian Church at Durham thinking seriously of disbanding, the attention of Rariton Presbytery was directed to this neighborhood as a rather promising one in which to organize a church. Accordingly Mr. Sherwood kept up preaching in it until probably 1847 when he made application to Presbytery requesting leave to erect a house of Worship and organize a Presbyterian Church within its bounds, in Holland, to be united for the time being with Milford Presbyterian Church. Presbytery granted the request at its April meeting in 1848. At this juncture the location of the house caused some friction. Several places were suggested—notably near the eight square school house and Gravel Hill. In favor of its present location it was urged among other reasons: (1) The land would be donated;(2) A foot bridge would probably be erected across the river at this point; (3) Monroe, Kintnersville, Durham Iron Works, Riegelsville and Durham Presbyterian Church about to cease. *All* these would be drawn here and constitute a large share of its support. But as all depended on the foot bridge when that went down—the *Pennsylvania support went with it.* The following paper was drawn up and started out June 3,1848:

"We, the subscribers, will pay the sums annexed to our names for the purpose of erecting a Presbyterian Church in Holland on ground to be given by John Tomson, near Tomson's Ferry; and also to purchase a public burying ground adjoining the said lot for the benefit of all denominations; the church and premises to be under the control of that branch of "the Presbyterian Church in the United States whose General Assembly meets annually."

A sufficient amount being subscribed to warrant the undertaking it was next deemed advisable to effect a legal organization of the church, and accordingly notices were posted, trustees chosen, a deed of incorporation executed and the usual oaths subscribed, copies of which are here given, as follows:

"Notice! The religious Society or Congregation of Christians called Presbyterians of Holland and vicinity, in Hunterdon county, New Jersey, attached to the General Assembly of the Presbyterian Church (usually called Old School Presbyterians) are hereby notified to meet at the house of John Tomson, near Tomson's Ferry, on Saturday, the 22nd of July next, at two o'clock p. m., for the purpose of electing trustees of said Congregation or Society with a view of incorporating the same agreeably to law."

	John Bloom
	John Tomson
July 10, 1848	Michael Fraley, Jun

Deed. "To all whom it may concern:
Know ye that at a public meeting of the religious Society, or Congregation of Christians, called Presbyterians, attached to the General Assembly of the Presbyterian Church of the United States (usually called Old School Presbyterians) assembled at the house of John Tomson, near Tomson's Ferry, in Holland, in the township of Alexandria, county of Hunterdon, and State of New Jersey, on the twenty-second day of July. In the year of our Lord one thousand eight hundred and forty-eight, in pursuance of an advertisement set up in open view on the door of said John Tomson's public house, giving at least ten days' notice of the time and purpose of assembling: We, John Bloom, John Tomson, John H. Johnson, Benjamin Snider, and Michael Fraley, Jun., were by a plurality of voices of said Society or Congregation then present duly elected Trustees of said religious Society, agreeably to the act of Assembly of said State, in such cases made and provided. And we, the said Trustees elected as aforesaid, having assembled at the time and place aforesaid, and having each of us taken and subscribed before William Egbert, Esquire, a Justice of the Peace in and for said county of Hunterdon, the oath to support the constitution of the United States; the oath of allegiance prescribed by law; and an oath for the faithful execution of trust reposed in him as Trustee as aforesaid, according to the best of his abilities and understanding, did take upon ourselves and said religious Society or Congregation the name of THE FIRST PRESBYTERIAN CHURCH OF HOLLAND, all of which facts we do hereby certify and signify.

In witness whereof, we have hereonto set our hands and affixed our seals, at the place aforesaid, the day and year written above.

John Bloom   {seal}
John Tomson   {seal}
John H. Johnson   {seal}
Benjamin Snider   {seal}
Michael Fraley, Jun. {seal}

Signed sealed and delivered in the presence of

William Egbert.

STATE OF NEW JERSEY, }ss.
    HUNTERDON CO.

Before me, William Egbert, one of the Judges of the Inferior Court of Common Pleas, in and for said county, on the ninth day of September in the year of our Lord one thousand eight hundred and forty-eight, personally appeared John Bloom, John Tomson, John H. Johnson, Benjamin Snider, and Michael Fraley, Jun., known to me to be the grantors of the above deed of incorporation, to whom I made known the contents thereof; and who acknowledged that they signed, sealed and delivered the same as their voluntary act and deed for the uses and purposes therein expressed. All of which is certified by

WILLIAM EGBERT

Recorded in the Clerk's office in Flemington, Oct. 5th, 1848, in vol. 5 special deeds, Fol. 40 and 41.

The following oaths were taken and subscribed by each Trustee:

STATE OF NEW JERSEY, }ss.
    HUNTERDON CO.

I, Michael Fraley, Jr., do sincerely profess and swear that I do and will bear true and faithful allegiance to the government established in this State under the authority of the people, so help me God. And further swear that I will (as Trustee) of the First Presbyterian Church of Holland, faithfully perform and execute the trust reposed in me as Trustee as aforesaid, according to the best of my ability and understanding, so help me God. And also do solemnly swear that I will support the

Constitution of the United States, so help me God.

MICHAEL FRALEY, JUN.

Sworn and subscribed this 9th day of September A .D. 1848, before me one of Justices of the Peace in and for said county of Hunterdon.

WILLIAM EGBERT

Accordingly measures were soon thereafter taken to build a house of worship and in the Fall of the same year work on the building was commenced under the supervision of the Trustees. The masonry was done by Alban White and the carpenter work by Michael Fraley (trustee). The house was completed and dedicated in the Fall or early Winter 1849.

[TO BE CONTINUED]

Figure 12.   Holland Presbyterian Church.   Photo courtesy of Lawrence LaFevre.

We now have in its history the rather strange anomaly of a house of worship built and dedicated and no church organized to occupy it and not more than half a dozen Presbyterians to constitute a church of. However Mr. Sherwood had faith in the enterprise and continued preaching in the new house until the following June at which time he requested the Session of Milford Presbyterian Church to meet in Holland Church. The following minute of that meeting entered in Milford session book is here given as a matter of interest as well as being the first sessional meeting held in the Holland Church:

June 29th, 1850

"Session met after preparatory lecture held in Holland Church and was constituted by prayer. Present, J. H. Sherwood, Moderator; George Carpenter and Joseph Hunt, Elders. Jesse Sinclair and wife Catharine, John Bloom and wife Hannah, and John Tomson, presented themselves for examination and were received into the communion of this (Milford) Church. There being no further business Session adjourned. Concluded with prayer."

These newly received members together with nine others—fourteen in all—withdrew from Milford Presbyterian Church Nov. 14th, 1850, and on the same day were constituted the *First Presbyterian Church of Holland* by a committee of the Presbytery of Rariton, composed of Dr. Jacob Kirkpatrick, Dr. P. O. Stoddiford, and Rev. Samuel F. Porter. The names of the constituent members were: Sarah Elliot, Catharine Welch, wife of Abner Welch; Rebecca Tomson, Lettitia VanCamp, Margaret Rapp (Vanarsdale); Mary A. Snider, Benjamin Snider, Rebecca Snider his wife; John Tomson, John Bloom, Hannah Bloom his wife; Jesse Sinclair, Catharine Sinclair his wife; and Hannah Wright. But two of these—Mrs Vanarsdale and the writer are now living. Mrs. Vanarsdale united with Milford Church March 13th, 1847. Benjamin Snider and Jesse Sinclair were chosen first Elders; Rev. J. H. Sherwood installed first pastor, and

89

served until his death in 1854. He was succeeded by Rev. Peter Augustus Stoddiford in 1855.

I have now completed as best I could from memory the sketch proposed at the beginning. The bi-centennial of the church will occur in the year 1900, when doubtless the event will be celebrated, and its subsequent history since the organization also written. For the gratification of those who may pass away before that event occurs, I will append hereto a condensed statement of ministers and officers who have served the Church since its organization:

Ministers— J. H. Sherwood, 1850 to 1854; P. A. Stoddiford, 1855 to 1859; James Lewers, 1860 to 1865; A. H. Sloat, 1865 to 1867; J. Burroughs, 1868 to 1878; I. M. Paterson, 1878 to 1888; B. G. VanCleve, present pastor since 1889.

Ruling Elders—Benjamin Snider, Jesse Sinclair, Wm. Quick, John D. Bloom, Stephen Bennett, Peter Snider, D. R. Bloom, Peter Rapp, and S. D. Sinclair.

Trustees—John Tomson, John H. Johnson, John Bloom, Benjamin Snider, Michael Fraley, Duvilious Vanderbelt, George W. Hager, Jonas Rapp, John Snider, Peter Snider, Samuel Vansealous, and George W. Snider.

Total membership, 211.

Children baptized, 49

I may have erred in the giving of some dates in the foregoing sketch, but otherwise think it will be found substantially correct.

▦ REMINISCENES ▦

From the Hunterdon Independent 1896
Found in the Srope Scrapbooks at the Hunterdon County
Historical Society

Reminiscenes   by Jesse Sinclair

The "Hunterdon Independent," Jan. 17, contains
an interesting letter relating to a friendly visit made by J.
W. L. to his only living teacher, Barzilla Williams, to whom
he went to school in 1836, in Spring Hill school house.
The letter in question has revived some recollections of the
same period and neighborhood, which, with the editor's
permission, I will write for the paper.
In early life I took a fancy to school teaching, and
accordingly chose it for a profession; which I pursued ten
years and then gave it up—it then being an unpopular
and non paying business.
In the winter of 1835-6 and 1837-7 I was engaged
as an assistant teacher by my cousin John B. Sinclair—
then teaching in what is now Kingwood School District No.
33. Thus it happened that while my friend J. W. L. was
attending Barzilla Williams' school at Spring Hill in 1836 I
was in a neighboring district qualifying myself for the
duties of my chosen profession.

I remember very well Barzilla Williams teaching at Spring Hill in 1836 and also remember that when Mr. Williams left there my cousin had a mind to apply for the situation; but the trustees (of said now No. 33) opposed it and he changed his mind and staid where he was. I may say in passing that I had previously been a pupil of Barzilla's brother, James Williams, who had taught in Holland.

The school house, in which my cousin was then teaching was a frame building and stood beside the road leading from Frenchtown to Baptisttown on ground probably once a part of then Moses Roberson's land. On three sides of the interior strips of timber were fastened in the wall upon which boards were laid for writing tables. Benches made of slabs were used for seats. I remember in 1835, several broken benches were replaced with pine slabs brought from Godfrey Case's saw mill. The teacher sat on a chair with a sheepskin cushion and had a writing desk standing on a saw buck legs— these with a ten plate stove made up the furniture. Adjoining the house there was a grove of white oak and hickory trees standing. In those days, schools were supported by voluntary subscriptions. The usual price paid per scholar was $2 for 72 days instruction. Many schools were closed during the greater part of the spring, summer and fall months, the children being kept home at an early age to work. But in the winter *all*, big and little, attended school. And as there were nearly as many different text books as children it is easy to see why an assistant teacher was required; and also the necessity of keeping the children in school from sun up to sun down—no five or six hour days then—nor any softening of the brains of children, either, on account of over study; though a scholar caught with his or her eyes off their books longer than half a minute was sure to get a whack. It also required much of the teacher's time to make and repair goose quill pens—steel pens being then unknown in the schools.

In the winter of 1835-6 I boarded with aunt Sallie McPeck, who lived in a log house standing near the Nichisakawick creek and junction of the roads leading to Baptisttown and Barbertown; a stone house now occupies the site. I don't know who lives in it. Mrs. McPeck was a daughter of Nathaniel Thatcher and Lorana Taylor. She had married one, Daniel McPeck, who was then dead. I know nothing of his ancestry. Their children were, Daniel, who had left home; Thatcher, who lived with his mother and worked at shoemaking; Nathaniel, also from home; Bartholomew, who came now and then a day to school; Lydia Ann, wife of Peter Bellis; Mary, who was afterward twice married; first to Joseph Slack, second husband Francis R. Horner, and Julian, who also came to school.

In the following winter 1836-7, I boarded with Mrs. Grace Roberson, widow of John Roberson. Her maiden name was Opdyke—and was maternally descended from the Everett family. She lived on the Ridge road, and had children: Daniel, Samuel, Lavina, Catharine, Mershon, Mary and Elizabeth. The three latter only were home that winter. Mershon afterward married a daughter of Samuel Eichlin and Ruth Purcell, and I think Elizabeth became the wife of a Brink and was the mother of Sallie Brink, who was married to William Sinclair of Holland. Both Mrs. Roberson and Mrs. McPeck were good to me, and their memories and kind acts are still cherished and held in grateful remembrance.

Writing thus far has been to me a pleasant entertainment. But a feeling of sadness comes to me now as I think of the house and the roads and patrons of that school all gone from earth; and the children crowded within its walls sixty years ago nearly all gone too—yes, I am sad.

"A few more short years shall roll
A few more seasons come,
And all shall be with those that rest
Asleep—within the tomb."

J. S.

Figure 13. Another view of the Jesse Sinclair home. The family in the picture is the Birkner family who lived in the house in the 1930's. Photo courtesy of the Birkner family.

HISTORY OF HOLLAND SCHOOL
BY JESSE SINCLAIR

From: The Milford Leader   **Whole No. 913**
Thursday, Sept. 23, 1897   **(Part 1)**

Holland School No. 20, (prior to 1867 known as
No. 2) is bounded North by Mount Joy and Finesville
School Districts; East by Spring Mills; and South and
West by the Delaware River. It embraces within its limits
considerable territory, which at the time of its organization
was a part of a large tract of land owned by Sir Robert
Barker, of Bushbridge, England, and like many other
lands in Hunterdon county held in large tracts, was leased
for a term of years to the first settlers thereon.

Peter Cincleare (Sinclair) settled within the District
in 1753 and was one of Barker's tenants for thirty-one
years. Henry Snider came to it in 1766 and was also a
tenant of Barker for twenty-seven years. And it is quite
certain that other, both before and after these periods,
must have settled here the same way; as in the opening of
the present century the land was well cleared and
presented in that respect much the same appearance then
as now. But these, merely renters, having left no records
of their sojourn here cannot be traced with any certainty.
It is supposed, however, they had children to educate and
a school to do it in; and accordingly a fairly well supported
tradition maintains that the first School in Holland was

95

kept in a house then standing where George W. and
Mahlon Hager's barn yard now is. Peter Tinsman, born in
1774, when ninety years old stood in this barn yard where
the foundation of some building is yet visible, and in the
presence of George W. Hager told his father, (George
Hager), that on this foundation, yet visible, a house once
stood in which he went to school when young. Previous to
this the elder children of George Hager, Sr., when young,
had frequently picked up about the place broken slate
pencils and wondered how they came there. Moreover, it
is known that some at least, and doubtless all of Henry
Snider's eleven children born between 1757 and 1782
could read, write and cipher fairly well, which, taken in
connection with the traditions and other circumstances
referred to, seem to indicate the existence of a school in
Holland as early at least, if not before, the Revolutionary
War. It would now be a matter of great interest to us if
Mr. Tinsman had told us the name of the teacher to whom
he here went to school. Assuming this house and place to
have been the first where a school was kept in Holland, we
find the second house to have been built about 1790. It
was a log house located some fifty yards East of where the
present house stands on grounds of said Barker, held
under a lease with reversion of land when the house
should cease to be used for school purposes. In 1794 the
land on which it stood, with other lands, was sold to
James Burson. In 1809 Burson conveyed it to John
Eichlin. It is now owned by Jacob Robbins.

Among the owners and renters of the lands and
probable supporters of the school prior to 1800, are found
the names of Joseph and James Burson; Henry, Jacob
and Martin Snider, Christian and Andrew Roup; Frederic
Trauger, William Shearer, _____Shannon, Joseph
Loughley, Henry Mettler, Thomas Purcell, Johnston
Cornell, Henry Stoll, Jacob Vanderbilt, Francis Wade,
John Pennwell, James Davis. Between 1800 and 1810 the
following changes occurred: James Burson sold to John
Eichlin; Joseph Burson to John Angell and William
Posten; Frederic Trauger to John Moore; Loughley to
Jeremiah Clark; _____Shannon to Philip H. Rapp;
Shearer to Michael Fraley; Francis Wade to John Hager,
Joseph Godley and Jacob Crouse; Penwell to Philip
Burgstresser; Cornell to John Fisher; Henry Mettler to
Michael Fackenthall, and Davis to John Sinclair. After

1816 the log house ceased to be used for school purposes and the land lapsed.

Tradition gives the names of four teachers that taught in the log house – Daniel S. Moore, Jasper Royce, James R. Albach, and George Ellicott.

Daniel S. Moore was of Irish descent and was a pettifogger as well as a teacher. He married Elsie Stoll; owned the lot late John P. Quick's. It was sold from him by the Sheriff in 1821 in consequence of his having become security on a note for $225.

Jasper Royce was a Yankee; married Elizabeth Snyder (nee Sinclair), settled on the farm late Henry Super's. Sixty-two years ago removed to Ashtabula county, Ohio, where he died.

James R. Albach was the nephew of John Sinclair and but sixteen years old when he taught in the log house. He also removed West, to Butler county, Ohio, where in 1858 he compiled and published a history of the Western States, and died unmarried.

George Ellicott became a veteran; was the last to teach in the second house and the first teacher in the third house. He also taught in the third house in 1839 and again, in 18860 [sic], comprising a period of forty-five years between his entry and exit into and out of Holland.

From The Milford Leader   Whole No. 914
Thursday, September 30, 1897   (Part 2)

Holland School
By Jesse Sinclair

On the 14th day of June, 1817, John Sinclair conveyed to Jacob Snider, John Eichlin, Phillip Burgstresser and Michael Fraley, (trustees), and to their successors in the same trust forever, eighteen hundred square feet of land, situate about fifty yards West of the log house, (for the purpose of building and maintaining a school thereon.) In July 1864, Christopher Hager conveyed to John H. Sinclair, Jesse Sinclair and Wilson Angell, (trustees), one hundred and twenty square feet of land for the use of said school. And again to the same use, January, 1876, Francis M. Hager and wife Catharine Ann, conveyed to Duvilious Vanderbilt, Godfrey Bellis and Hart Sinclair, (trustees), one hundred and thirty-three thousandths of an acre of land. On August 1ˢᵗ, 1884, Jacob Robbins conveyed to Wm. Rapp, David O. Hager and Urmston B. Hager, (trustees), the right to the use of water of a certain spring to be led through pipes laid underneath the ground to a point on the North side of the road leading, etc., for the use of said school.

It is supposed that at the founding of the Log House a "Nanny Berry Bush" had been planted nearby to furnish the teachers with rods to be used according to a custom prevalent in Solomon's day. The bush was a prolific one—some scholars fancied they could see the sprouts grow.

The third school house was built on the land above named in 1817. It was an octagonal stone structure and lasted about forty-seven years. The carpenter work was done by Joseph Rapp and the mason work (presumably) by Wm. Sinclair. The house was famous, not only as a place of learning, but also for preaching, singing schools, debating schools, shows and exhibitions, such as were common in olden times. The furniture of the house, apart from the seats, consisted of a teacher's desk and six other movable double desks in which the scholars' books were kept when not in use. The tops of these desks were semi-hexagonal in form, each having four lids hinged to them, which were used for writing upon. The six desks contained a writing surface sufficient to accommodate forty-eight pupils writing at the same time. They were also used as seats for visitors from Bunn Valley and other places attending our singing schools and such like. An old ten plate stove without side doors, named Reuben Trexler, cast at Mary Ann Furnace, Berks Co., Pa., (date not recalled) occupied the centre of the room. There were few school houses in that day better equipped for business than the dear old eight square.

At that period orthography, reading, writing and arithmetic were the only branches taught in common schools. These however appear to have been quite efficiently taught here, giving the school a good reputation abroad; hence pupils of other districts wishing to pursue the higher branches of mathematics-algebra, trigonometry, surveying, etc.—usually came to Holland to study them. In fact it was a sort of Seminary to which pupils of other districts frequently came to complete their education before going out into the world. We here recall a small class of such pupils consisting of John L. Riegel, Emmet Quin and John C. Purcell, who took a one or two year's course at "Holland Eight Square" and graduated in 1832. Afterwards John L. Riegel became an eminently successful business man; Emmet Quin a lawyer and John C. Purcell a medical doctor. There lies before me a splendid bit of penmanship written with a goose quill pen and reads as follows:

Received February 20th, 1833, of Samuel
Sinclair the sum of $2.85. It being for
tuition. (of the writer I suppose)
James Williams

In September, 1830, John Wesley Robbins and Hummer Bellis while at school, under a pear tree at noon recess, were struck by lightning and killed. The first Sunday-School of Holland was held in the Eight Square by D. U. Sheets in 1840. This house went down in 1864. To some in Holland its memory is still precious.

On Sept. 8th, 1863, the inhabitants of Holland met to consider the advisability of building a new house. The meeting voted aye unanimously. Met again on the 12th. Appointed Jacob Robbins, Wilson Angell and Jonas Rapp to ascertain cost of same, etc. Met the 18th. Appointed Wilson Angell to ask permission of Christopher Hager to unload building material on his premises; also to lead water across his land. Also appointed Wm. Quick and Jonas Rapp to make a draught of the house. Met the 21st. Requests of Mr. Hager reported granted. Draught deemed unnecessary. Met the 25th to receive bids for the mason work. The bids being deemed too high and Winter approaching, the matter was postponed till the following Spring. Meanwhile a building committee was formed consisting of Jacob Robbins, Wilson Angell and Elias M. Rapp, which on February 13th, 1864, entered into written contract with Fred Keller and Franklin Trauger, both of Bucks Co., Pa., to do the mason work of a two story stone house 24 feet by 36 feet, according to certain specifications for $205. The Committee at its own expense, to remove the old house, and prepare and deliver on the ground all necessary building material. John Kooker done the carpenter work. Whole cost of house not at hand at present.

The lower room is used for public school purposes exclusively. The upper room may be, and is used for preaching, Sunday-schools, singing schools, etc. The lower room was refurnished with the more modern seats and writing tables in 1864.

(to be continued)

Figure 14. Holland School built in 1864. Photo courtesy of Kathy Sciarello.

**From The Milford Leader   Whole No. 915
Thursday Oct. 7, 1897   (Part 3)**

Holland School
By Jesse Sinclair

There are no records of the trustees and teachers of this school extant prior to 1864, and those since then, so far as we have found them, very improperly kept. We shall therefore not attempt to give the names of trustees, other than those incidentally mentioned in the course of this writing. We have, however, with the aid of some friends exhumed from the buried past the following named teachers: (Order irregular and uncertain.)

Daniel S. Moore	Peter Snyder
Jasper Royce	Jesse Sinclair
James R. Albach	Moses Bateman
James Sage	W. W. Wort

Phillip Lippincott
David Williams
John Purcell
James Williams
Ezra Brewster
Jacob B. Curtis
————Pewters
John Holland
Judah Tancy
Daniel U. Sheets
George H. Michener
William Loder
John B. Sinclair
William G. Tomer
John H. Griffith
Ed. Shug
Elizabeth McNamoe
E. Bell
Edith Lowe
Phebe Reynalds
Charles B. Erwin
Israel Gray
J. D. Gray
L. S. Zinar
Francis Raub
C. Fackenthall
Annie Maurbon
Lafayette R. Amey
Newberry Deemer
Thos. R. Thatcher

John McMahn
Amy Royce
John W. Snyder
Mary Williams
Eliza Brough
Josiah Metz
Miss Ambler
Archibald Moore
————Johnson
Lewis Beals
George C. Landon
D. R. Williamson
Louisa Merrit
Charles Durbin
Newberry Crouse
John Hayes
Ella Miller
Francis Cressman
Matilda Fine
Charles Snider
Cora Rapp
Annie M. Hager
Millie Burwell
James Anderson
McClelland Moser
George Ellicott
Francis Pullis
————Lundy
Jacob Crouse

In looking over the above list of teachers more than one-half are known to have died. Of those yet living—some have married—or are engaged in other pursuits and callings. A few still have the harness on and are engaged teaching. Among those who have married, or entered into other pursuits, we note the following:

John Henry Griffith is a medical doctor practicing at Phillipsburg, N. J.

Louisa Merrit is the wife of Reading Bougher and resides at Rancocas, N. J.

Charles B. Erwin holds a responsible position with the P. R. R. Company at Jersey City, N. J.

Ella Miller is the wife of Howard Rapp residing in Washington, N. J.

Millie Burwell married Chas. Maddock and resides in Easton, Pa.

Geo. H. Michenor married Ann Sinclair a pupil of Holland School; became a lawyer; practiced at Doylestown, Pa.; died comparatively young, leaving a son, Harry C.— practicing in Philadelphia, Pa.

Wesley W. Wort also became a lawyer and practiced at Bloomsburg, Pa., where a few years ago he died.

Amy Royce, also deceased, was a daughter of Jasper Royce who taught in the Log school house.

William G. Tomer is the author of the music set to the hymn "God be with you till we meet again," now sung in all lands and in all tongues. He is at present editor of the Hunterdon Gazette. (Since deceased.—Ed.)

L. S. Zinar was a physician and practiced in South Easton, Pa. (Deceased.)

D. R. Williamson keeps a hardware store at Riegelsville, Pa.

Anna M. Hager is the wife of John Lewdrop, residing at Bloomsbury, N. J.

Cora Rapp is the wife of E. C. Severs living at Mount Pleasant, N. J.

Thos. R. Thatcher is a trucker in the "Hill Regions" of New Jersey.

Francis Pullis removed from Holland School to Mount Pleasant where one night he became badly frightened at an excavated pumpkin with a candle in it, from the effects of which he died shortly afterwards.

John Holland was an Irishman and chewed pig tail tobacco—big. One day Dan Bloom got over on the girl's side of the house where, of course, he had no business, and Johny gave him a touch or two of the Nanny Berry at which Dan laughed, whereupon Johny said, "D——n your soul and do you laff," and went at him again—this time more vigorously. The writer was a little mixed up in the fray and received two or three cuts—but he didn't laugh.

Mr. Pewters was an Englishman and wore knee breeches and governed his school by monitors. On opening school he would throw a stick, kept for the purpose, at the first one caught talking and call out his name, whose duty it was to pick it up, station himself upon a bench, keep watch until another talked to whom the stick was thrown, his name was called, whose duty it

likewise was to pick it up and take the place of the former and watch for another talker. One morning Francis M. Hager's tongue became unruly and he took his stand to make observations. He watched a long time and it did seem as though no one would ever talk again. However, at last, Wilson Angell leaned towards a boy to give him some instruction and Francis let drive and yelled out WILSON ANGELL; but Wilson paid no attention to it until after having been two or three times commanded by the teacher he picked up the stick and gave it to "Reuben Trexler" who soon devoured it, and Pewters henceforth governed his school somewhat after the manner of Johny Holland.
(to be continued)

From The Milford Leader   **Whole No. 916**
Thursday Oct. 14, 1897   **(Part 4)**

Holland School
By Jesse Sinclair

Daniel U. Sheets was a native of White House, N. J. He came to Holland in 1840. He introduced into the school several innovations, among them English grammar and geography, made a globe and blackboard, and taught elocution on account of which he was deemed by some a very great and wise man; others said he was a crank and a little up-set in his mind. This difference of opinion among the people regarding Mr. Sheets produced a wrangle which in 1841 terminated in a dissolution of the district into two parts—North and South. The South having declared her independence next set about building a house of her own, which was located on land of George Hager near Wm. Fraley's place. This house had a steeple and a bell—two more novelties in Holland. The bell, we learn, is still in existence and can be seen at George W. & Mahlon Hager's mill. While the new house was being built Mr. Sheets taught in a log dwelling house then standing on Phillip Rapp's land. There is a tradition that Phillip H. Rapp had previously taught in this log dwelling a free school. The writer's recollections of Mr. Sheets now is, that he was a good teacher and all right, only a little too radical for the people of Holland at that period. The separation lasted until 1863, when the two districts were again united and the present house built as a memorial of the reunion.

103

The following is a list of teachers that taught in South Holland school house:

Daniel U. Sheets	Egbert Loder
Fell R. Furman	Charles Myrick
George Wagner	Jonas Rapp
Edwin F. Bird	Alexander Holmes
A. H. Stover	Rebecca Loder
Wm. Dolton	Jacob Black
Benjamin Loder	------- Kitchen
Jesse Sinclair	Phillip Lippincott
Annie Hunt	Peter Snider
Jos. D. Burgstresser	Nathan Crouse
Elizabeth McNamee	Minnie Fackenthall
Joseph Cooley	Amy Johnson
John Patrick	Jacob Ely
John W. Snyder	William Evans
Carrie Fackenthall	David Donnelly

In about 1832 an event occurred that belongs to this history, which is here repeated, even at the risk of making it a "chestnut."

One day some tracts were left at the school for distribution among the scholars. Their distribution, however, was forbidden, and tracts fastened to a pole planted near the school house.

The people of the district were notified to appear at the place next day evening and witness the burning of them. Nearly all the district came. They were formed into line, and under command of Tunis Lippincott marched some distance to and fro and halted opposite the pole, where each took a drink of whiskey brought there by Thomas Craig, then living where Tomson Fine now resides. The tracts were then fired and burned, with loud cries against priestcraft and priest rule in this country. The writer, who was present both at the reception and burning of the tracts, always supposed they were published by the American Tract Society, but he has recently been shown one, said to have been picked up after the burning, which is a temperance tract published, if I remember correctly, at Boston, Mass. Many of the early settlers of Holland came from priest ridden countries, and always kept an eye on their movements in this country.

Prior to 1867 the public schools of Holland, as elsewhere, were maintained and paid for by the parents of the children attending them. Teachers often had a hard time of it. They were expected to open school early in the morning and close late in the afternoon; make and repair goose quill pens; board around; collect their own money; call two or three times for a fifty cent bill and never get it, the delinquent putting on the finishing touches by calling him a scamp too lazy to work.

Such is the history of Holland School as we have found it. We should like to know more of its history and with greater certainty, but all else seems hidden. Trusting what we have found may interest some that have been connected with this school, we close with somewhat of the feeling that it is the last history we shall ever again write for publication.

Jesse Sinclair

July 4th, 1896
[Ed. Note: Jesse Sinclair passed away September 13, 1896]

Figure 15. The interior of Holland School in 1900. Photo courtesy of Charlotte Wertz Garcia.

▓ MISCELLANEOUS SINCLAIR ▓ AND HOLLAND TOWNSHIP INFORMATION

[Editor's note: The following was found during a random ramble on the Internet during the researching of this paper. Coincidence or ?]

From: The Sinclair Family by Frances Cowles

At: http://sinclair.quarterman.org/cowles.html

Not all the Sinclairs in America, however are of Norman stock. Some of them came from Germany. One family of German descent lives in New Jersey, and was founded there at New Holland by Peter Cincleare, who chose yet another way of spelling this variously spelled name. He was born in Germany in 1719, and arrived in Philadelphia in 1753 in the St. Michael, from Hamburg. He settled on a tract of some eight thousand acres of land and for thirty-one years worked the ground as a renter. He had three children, John, Peter, and Mary.

John, born in Germany in 1743, eleven years before his father came to America, bought the property his father had worked, and additional lands at New Holland, and became a prosperous farmer. He served as a teamster in the Revolutionary war. His wife was Anna Ahlbach, or

Alpock, daughter of Johan, who came from Holland in the Hope in 1743. John's son Samuel also married a young woman of Dutch descent, Permelia Vancamp, and Samuel's son, Jesse Sinclair, teacher, farmer and man of affairs, married for his first wife Catherine Welsh, also of Dutch descent.

In early days the name was variously spelled, Sinclare, Sinkler, Sinklaire, Sinclair and St. Clair; in the case of the German Peter, Cincleare. Nowadays it is generally spelled either St. Clair or Sinclair, although in parts of Virginia Sinklers are still found.

[Editor's note: The following articles describe the tragic accident and slow recovery that befell Jesse Sinclair in 1889]

**From The Milford Leader   Whole No. 493
Thursday August 22, 1889**

Correspondents Section – Holland
The many friends of Squire Jesse Sinclair ("Musconetcong"), of the hill regions, will regret to hear of an unfortunate accident which befell him Wednesday afternoon of last week. He had taken a lot of peaches from his place over to Simeon Sinclair's and on the way home a bolt came out of the tongue on one side of his truck wagon, causing the wagon to run up on the bank along the road. Mr. Sinclair was pitched out and was considerably injured by the fall. A boy was immediately dispatched for a doctor, but before help reached him the heavy shower of that afternoon came up and the squire lay for nearly half an hour in the terrific rainstorm. When he was taken home it was found that one side was entirely paralyzed and at this writing he is lying helpless in bed, although somewhat improved. "June Bug" sends his heartfelt sympathy to his old friend and sincerely trusts he will soon be able to be about again.   June Bug

[June Bug gave ongoing reports of Squire Sinclair's recovery progress in the **Holland Correspondents** column of The 'Leader' as follows:]
No. 495, 9/5/1889: 'Squire Sinclair continues to improve slowly.

No. 497, 9/19/1889: I regret to report that 'Squire Jesse Sinclair does not show any signs of improvement. He is still confined to his bed, utterly helpless, on account of the paralytic stroke recently received by him. Our prayer is that he may be again restored to his wonted strength.

No. 498, 9/26/1889: 'Squire Jesse Sinclair shows some signs of improvement now.

No. 499, 10/3/1889: Jesse Sinclair continues to improve.

No. 501, 10/17/1889: 'Squire Sinclair does not improve as fast as his friends would like. He is able to walk about the house with assistance, but does not seem to gain much in strength.

No. 506, 11/21/1889: 'Squire Sinclair continues to improve slowly.

No. 509, 12/12/1889: 'Squire Sinclair continues to improve, and I hope to see him around again before along. He has been terribly afflicted, but has borne it all with great patience and resignation.

No. 512, 1/2/1890: The holiday entertainment of the Holland Church, Saturday night, drew a full house, and the audience was more than delighted with the exercises. The programme included singing, recitations, dialogues, etc., and was rendered in a creditable manner to all taking part. "Santa Claus" was on hand as usual, and besides treating the scholars, many persons in the audience came in for a share of his gifts. 'Squire Sinclair, superintendent of the Sunday-school, and Stephen Bennett, assistant superintendent, were each presented with a fine turkey, while the pastor, Rev. Mr. VanCleve came in for a turkey and also a splendid cake baked as only our Holland ladies know how. There was no Christmas tree, but the church was appropriately decorated. No admission was charged, a collection being taken up to defray the expenses of the occasion. The entertainment was worthy an admission fee, as it was voted the best ever given at the church.

No. 515, 1/23/1890: 'Squire Sinclair is now able to be out a little, after his long illness, when the weather is nice.

From The Milford Leader   Whole No. 21
Thursday, August 5, 1880

Local Notices column:

Jesse Sinclair of Holland, and D. R. Hill of Alexandria, have been selected as part of a committee composed of one person from each township for the purpose of receiving and forwarding samples of fertilizers to Prof. Cook, of New Brunswick for analysis, the State having provided for such analysis at its own expense.

Samuel, a young son of Thomas Hunt, had the end of one of his toes taken off in a singular manner on Monday. He was playing with a large snapper which had been captured and fastened near the house, and to tease it stuck out his foot at the snapper's head, when it caught one of his toes in its mouth, taking the nail and the end of the toe completely off.

From: The Milford Leader
Thursday, September 17, 1896

Obituary

Jesse Sinclair died at his home on the Musconetcong Mountain about 11 o'clock last Sunday night. Deceased had been in ill health for a long time. Some seven years ago he was thrown from a peach wagon and sustained Injuries from which he never recovered and which kept him in doors most of the time. Being thus incapacitated from manual labor he took up for pastime study and research of historical matter, much of which was published In the columns of The Leader. Mr. Sinclair had just passed his 77th year and was highly esteemed and respected by all who knew him. He was Freeholder for one term and a Justice of the Peace for several years. He took a deep Interest in church work when his health permitted and was an Elder of the Holland Presbyterian church for many years. In his death the community has sustained a loss that each one sincerely mourns. Mr. Sinclair was twice married. His first wife was Miss Catharine Welch. Three children were born of their union, two of whom survive him. They are: Abner Sinclair, of Jersey City, and Miss Emma Sinclair who resides at home. His second wife also survives him. His funeral took place from his late residence yesterday (Wednesday) morning at 10:30 o'clock, Rev. Horace D. Sassaman of Mt. Pleasant, officiating. Interment in cemetery adjoining the Holland Church.

June Bug

From: The Democrat – Advertiser
Friday, September 25, 1896

Obituary

Jesse Sinclair, an old resident of Holland Township, died on Sunday night, 13th inst., at the age of 77 years. Mr. Sinclair was thrown from a wagon seven years ago, and sustained injuries from which he never recovered. He was a highly respected citizen, and a local historian of some note. He was a Freeholder from Holland township at one time and had been Justice of the Peace for several years.

From: The Hunterdon Independent
Friday September 18, 1896   page 3.

Obituary

Jesse Sinclair, residing in Holland Township, well known to many people in this place, died on Sunday night last at the age of 77 years. Mr. Sinclair was thrown from a wagon seven years ago, and sustained injuries from which he never recovered. He was a highly respected citizen and a local historian of some note.

Srope Scrapbook Vol. 40, page 336
Drafted – Civil War list – 1864
    Alexandria Township
        Theodore Sinclair
        William Sinclair
        Jesse Sinclair

Srope Scrapbook Vol. 38
Page 10:
1879 Appointments of Commissioners of deeds.
Holland Township
    Jesse Sinclair
    James C. Robbins

From: **Srope Scrapbook**
1880 Census report

Chas. A. Roberson, enumerator for Holland township hands us the following extract of the report of the township:

Population of Township	1887
Population of Milford	614
No. of Families in Township	427
No. of Houses in Township	411
No. of Farms in Township	170

No. of saw mills, 4; slaughter houses,1; boot and shoe factories, 2; stone quarries, 2; manufactories, 9, (including Warren Paper Mill which is enumerated in this township;) flour and grist mills, 5; No. of deaths, 24.

Page 250:
1880 – Holland Items
The annual election of officers of the Presbyterian Sabbath School was held on Sunday. The officers being as follows: Superintendent - Jesse Sinclair, Vice Superintendent - Stephen Bennett, Secretary – W. B. Hager, Treasurer – Peter Snyder, Librarian – J. W. Angel.
Page 379:
Marriages – 1874
Sinclair – Snyder – in Milford, Hunterdon County, August 8, by Rev. B. F. Summerbell, Jesse Sinclair of Holland, to Amy, daughter of Jacob Snyder, of Kingwood Township.
page 528:
An article on the proposed formation of the Hunterdon County Historical Society – 1885 mentions Jesse Sinclair as interested from Milford and Riegelsville.

From: The Milford Leader

Obituary

Mrs. Amy Sinclair
Widow of the late Jesse Sinclair, died at her home in Milford on Monday morning, Jan 29th, 1900, about 7:30 o'clock. Deceased had been in declining health for some time and for the past three months had been bedfast. Mrs. Sinclair's maiden name was Snyder and she was born in Holland, N.J., April 29, 1829, and was therefore aged 70 years and 9 months at the time of her demise. Besides Miss Emma Sinclair, who resided with

her and gave her every attention during her late sickness, and Abner Sinclair, of Jersey City, there survive her a stepson and daughter, Wilson West, of Bushnell, Ill., and Mrs. Jno. Hunt, of Chicago, Ill. Also three sisters and two brothers, viz: Mrs. Catharine Roberts and Miss Margaret Snyder, of Riegelsville, Pa.; Mrs. John Hunt, of Riegelsville, N.J.; John Snyder, of Baptisttown, and Levi Snyder, of Rosemont, N.J. Mrs. Sinclair has for many years been a consistent member of the Milford Christian Church. The funeral services will be held at her late residence this (Wednesday) afternoon at 2:30 o'clock conducted by Rev. W. Parkison Chase assisted by Rev. Robt. I. Gamon. Interment at Frenchtown. (1900)

**From: The Milford Leader   Whole No. 472
Thursday, March 28, 1889**

News of Holland by June Bug

Holland

John Clark, of High Bridge, is Jas. Iliff's new farm hand. Mr. Urmston B. Hager and family were up from Trenton over Sunday. S. D. Sinclair was elected trustee at the school meeting Tuesday evening of last week. Miss Jennie Phillips has been elected organist of the Union service at the schoolhouse. Mr. L. A. Butler and family, of Newark visited friends here for several days last week W. S. Voorhies, a Princeton Seminary student, will preach at the church Sunday afternoon. Wm. Laubach will move on Saturday next to Isaac S. Laubach's farm, above Finesville.

Mrs. Wm. Fraley, who has been visiting friends In Easton and Mauch Chunk for two weeks, has returned home.

A surveying party from Lambertville were engaged In looking up the line stones between Holland and Durham last week. Jos. Echlin, who has been down for some time with inflammatory rheumatism, does not improve any. He is bedfast and helpless. The property of Mrs. Mary Ann Van Camp, consisting of house and lot, was bid up to $300 at the sale on Tuesday, but was not sold. Rumor has it that James Draffin, who has been off duty for some time on account of a broken leg, will again take his old place as boss on section No. 8 on Monday.

Tuesday was a good day for movings up this way. Wm. Vanderbilt moved from the "Corner" to Edward Nolf's farm, vacated by Jacob Clark, who took possession of Andrew Cole's place. Andrew Cole and Alonzo Sinclair moved to Milford.

Ten shares of stock of the First National Bank of Easton, belonging to the estate of the late Abraham Fraley, were sold by the administrator on Wednesday of last week at the Lee House, Phillipsburg, to Mrs. Wilson Angel, for $94 per share.

A couple of tramps-male and female-were observed near the "crossroads" Sunday camping out. They did their washing in the creek; and performed other acts pertaining to a nomadic career. Who they were and where they hailed from, is a mystery.

A couple of boys on the mountain-Jonas Sinclair and Case Vanderbilt-took it into their heads to run away last week, and it is supposed they have gone West. No tidings have been heard from them since their disappearance, but it may be that they will yet return, like the prodigal, and be sorry for their foolishness.

A couple of our Holland citizens had an exciting experience the other evening. They had retired for the night and were about surrendering themselves into the arms of Morpheus when suddenly one side of the bed broke down and one of the occupants was out on the floor, he having jumped just in time. Pleased to state that neither was much injured, but terribly scared.
JUNE BUG.

**From The Milford Leader   Whole No. 845
Thursday, June 4, 1896**

Correspondents – Holland

Jeremiah Clark lost a cow and Wm. Rapp a horse the past week.

Services at the church was largely attended Sunday afternoon.

The strawberry crop will not be a very large one as the vines are not very full.

A. S. Knect and wife, of Easton, were among our visitors Sunday

During the heavy rain and wind storm last Thursday afternoon what might be termed a cyclone struck the twenty acre timber tract of Patrick McEntee in Pa., across the river from this place doing $1000 damage to it by twisting and breaking it off. Heavy damage was also done to Owen Stover's lot. It partially unroofed the school house at that point taking off one half of the roof on each side of the building. It then crossed the river to New Jersey throwing a tree across the telegraph wires; it then struck Patrick Feely's lot blowing all his apple and other trees down and moved his barn about a foot. It next visited William Phillips, F. M. Hager, A. C. Rapp, Wilson Angel, Hart Sinclair, G. W. & M. Hager, Mrs. Eliza Ulmer and others, doing several thousand dollars damage to property. Its direction was northerly and it moved over the top of Gravel Hill. Shingles from the Stover's school house were found on top of Gravel Hill, a distance of several miles. The rain also washed and did considerable damage to the corn fields in this section.

June Bug

From The Milford Leader   Whole No. 895
Thursday, May 20, 1897

Our Correspondents Column:
Holland

Rev. W. P. Chase will preach at the school house next Sunday afternoon at 2:30 o'clock.

Mrs. Jeremiah Clark who has been sick for some time with dropsy and brain trouble does not make much improvement.

Our truckmen are putting out large patches of cantaloupes, fifty and sixty thousand hills having been planted. This looks as though they might over stock the market.

Rapp & Sigafoos moved their steam saw mill the past week from Beaver Dam, Pa., to the lot of Patrick Feeley and will drag their logs from the mountain to the mill.

The convention of the Sunday schools comprising Alexandria, Holland and Frenchtown will convene at the

Presbyterian Church here on Wednesday of next week. An interesting program is in preparation. The up train leaving Milford at 9.10 A.M. and 2.15 P.M. and the train passing Holland about 3.45 down, will stop at the crossing near the church.

June Bug

Local Paper – 1872
Burglary — the house of Simeon D. Sinclair, at Musconetcong, was again entered by some scamp a short time ago, robbing it of whatever flour, sugar and coffee it contained, which however, did not prove to be a very large quantity. This place has for years been subject to sort of periodical visits of this kind, taking therefrom such articles as butter, lard, flour, and provisions generally. Would it not be well to stop right here? As it is possible the little perpetrator of these little deeds might yet run against a little snag.

S.

Obituary:
Died   1871
Aug 21st, near Riegelsville, Lizzie, daughter of Jesse Sinclair, aged about 14 years.

New Jersey's Old Holland
(Correspondent of Hunterdon Republican)
The original Holland had for its eastern boundary a cone-shaped elevation of land about four hundred feet high, called "Gravel Hill." From time immemorial it has been well covered with timber, and in later times supposed by some to contain coal. After James Parker had divided his large tract of land in Holland into modern sized farms, in 1793, he sent his surveyor, Edward Welsted, into "Gravel Hill" to partition it into wood lots, which were attached to and sold with the Holland and other surrounding farms; and thither the purchasers have since gone for a period of one hundred years to cut firewood. Probably two hundred years ago the Indians cleared about four acres on its summit, now called the "old field," which

they farmed until about 1740 or 1750, and then left it to the white men, who have since cultivated it down to the present time. Prior to 1830 a man named Adam Reifner lived up there, and died of cancer. The "Old Field" is now owned by Wm. Hager, and contains in part an apple orchard and other fruit trees, and presents a picturesque appearance amid the surrounding forest trees. For the past three or four years the woodsmen's axes have been lifted up against the trees of the hill, which now are fast disappearing. (1893)

▓ ARTICLE READ BEFORE THE ▓
HUNTERDON HISTORICAL SOCIETY
JESSE SINCLAIR MEMOIR
JULY 10, 1897
BY JOHN W. LEQUEAR

Dr. Samuel Johnson has said that no man has
ever resided in the world whose life properly written would
not be of advantage. It is with the utmost pleasure I sit
down to write a short sketch of the life of our deceased
brother Jesse Sinclair, who was born among the rugged
hills of the Mononghehala [Musconetcong] range of
mountains in the northern part of Hunterdon County.

He was born August 15th 1819 on the same farm
on which his father was born and spent his life and here
Jesse spent most of his life and died September 13th 1896
aged 77 years 29 days. We judge from the long huge rows
of stones heaped up along the fences the first labor of his
boyhood must have been picking stones, his youth was
spent at home with his father, as he was of a robust
constitution and industrious he as oportunity [sic] offered
engaged to work for the neighboring farmers and in
tending a sawmill, having a taste for knowledge and a love
of reading he endeavored to acquire as good an education

as the country schools afforded, and to improve this he taught school a number of quarters in Holland township, and at one time taught a school near Baptisttown, have often heard him express his regret that during his young manhood he acquired, like many other young men of that day, a taste for strong drink, that was likely to prove his ruin, but through the grace of God he was enabled to break away from this pernicious habit and become a strict temperance man, and a strong advocate in the temperance cause, he also acquired a knowledge of vocal music that enabled him to teach vocal music to the young people on the mountain. I was shown a small melodeon that was first introduced by Magor Rodgers about the year 1845, and which Mr. Sinclair carried about with him to assist him in his services. On the organization of the Holland Presbyterian church he became a leader of the singing, and was chosen superintendent of their Sunday School, and was continued so long as he was able to attend there he was a chosen elder of that church so long as he lived, he also took a deep interest in the Sunday school cause. I was secretary of the Hunterdon County SS Association for sixteen years, and we always expected him at our annual Convention and nearly always did meet him there, and always ready to take an active part in the services; when the beautiful hymn.

"I will sing you a song of that beautiful land,
The far away home of the Soul,
Where no storms ever beat on the glittering strand,
While the years of eternity roll."

Can well remember with what ernestness [sic] he joined in the singing of it. He served a term on the board of freeholders and proved himself a wise and judicious member of that board. He was also repeatedly elected a Justice of the peace in Holland township and discharged the duties of the office with fidelity, without fear or favor.

He soon after the formation of our Historical Society became a member of it. I believe he has never prepared a paper to be read before the society. Yet he has been diligent in searching and collecting materials of a historical nature that have assisted others and he has written a historical account of the early settlers of Holland Township and of the Hunt family, Moore, Williams, Rapp and other prominent families which he has published in the Milford Leader he has also written a history of the Holland township schools.

Jesse was the son of Samuel Sinclair and Amelia [Permelia] Vancamp and Nov. 2d 1848 married Catharine Welch, their children were Samuel born Jan. 12th 1850 died May 8th 1856. Anna Mary born March 24th 1852 died Mar. 30th 1854. Abner born April 20th 1855 living in New York. Elizabeth born Feb 3d 1858 died Aug. 21st 1871.

Infant born Dec. 9th 1860 died Dec 12 1860. Elmer E. born April 25th 1863 died July 15 1863. William Walter born Sept. 5th 1864 died Dec 21 1885. Emma Catharine born April 28th 1867 still living. He then mar[ried] Amy daughter of Jacob Snyder Aug. 8th 1874. They had no children. About seven years before his death he was driving along the road with two horses to a truck wagon standing up when the attachment of the tongue gave way one side and the wagon running out of the road up a bank he was pitched out and falling on a rock his spine was injured and he became a helpless invalid for the remainder of his life unable to leave home and requiring the attentions of his wife and daughter yet he bore it all patiently and resigned; it was one of the regrets of my life that I allowed him to suffer pain and confinement for these seven years and never visited him although assured my visits would have been so acceptable. A distinguished physician who attended him remarked if he should die and go to Heaven there was one man he expected to meet and that man was Jesse Sinclair. He has left an autobiographical sketch of his of his [sic] religious experience which will be appended to this and read thou[gh] there are some things that may seem to repeat what has been written in this.

Some reminescenes of my Religious Life

It is both interesting and profitable to often review their past religious experiences, and to note as far as they can, the first beginnings of God's dealings with their souls and the ways in which he has led them through this wilderness world. It is therefore my purpose in what follows to give a rough and brief sketch of my religious life, and some of the ways by which I have been led therein. And in the relation of which I remark first that I was born

121

on Sunday August 15th 1819 in what is now Holland township Hunterdon County New Jersey. I scarcely remember the time when I did not have religious impressions. I remember very well when I was not more than five years old that I had a very clear and distinct sense of right and wrong, with strong moral feelings of approval and disapproval. At this time neither of my parents were professors of religion and therefore rarely talked on religious subjects, though they often gave me good advice, as to this world and seemed desirous of making something out of me. And while I may not now remember it, yet I think they must have taught me some religious truths, for when I was about eight to nine years old I commenced praying occasionly [sic], especially when I was in any great trouble and some of these seem to have been answered, at least the things prayed for turned out as I wanted them to. Of course I did not then think myself a Christian, indeed I knew I was not, nevertheless during these early years of my life my conscience was active and keen, always approving the right and disapproving the wrong doings of my life as I understood right and wrong actions to be. Upon arriving at about the age of twelve or thirteen years Judge Philip Fine a prominent citizen and business man of Finesville, insisted upon loaning me two large sized volumes consisting of John Newton's letters or sermons, and afterwards Dick's Celestial Astronomy consisting of two good sized volumes, also, which I accepted and read with considerable interest, although much of what they contained was above my comprehension. About this time I also read Doddrige's rise and Progess [The Rise and Progress of Religion in the Soul] and Baxters call to the unconverted [A Call to the Unconverted], these latter books belonged to my aunt Letitia Van Camp who then had her home with my parents and took much interest in me: the reading of these writing at that early period of my life tended not only to keep the subject of religion before my mind, but also made it easy for me to embrace what the old devines called the Orthodox faith and doctrines. During the reading of these books, and afterwards I felt myself more and more a sinner in the sight of God, and was at times greatly troubled on account of it, and often wished I was a Christian. But as in those days it was hardly expected that one so young as I should be a Christian it made it easier for me to put the matter off until I should become older. When about thirteen years old my mother professed conversion and joined the Christian Church. She had formerly been a great singer of secular songs, but she now abandoned these and became equally great in sacred songs, now putting her entire soul into her singing of religious hymns as she had formerly done in secular ballads. Her singing often made one long to be a Christian too. Among her favorite hymns were "Oh how happy are they" "How tedious and tasteless the hours" etc the former being sung when her Christian hopes were bright. The latter when they were cloudy. As I write these things I also recall how often Mrs. Daniel Hart, Rosana Sailor, Maria Sailor, Elizabeth Dolton from Finesville with others would meet at our house on a Sunday morning and Mother and I with others would join them and march off on foot to the Milford Christian Church, at that time this was the only church at Milford or nearer than Mount Pleasant, neither were there any buggies or spring wagons in use, such as now, and the people either walked to church or rode on boulster wagons or on horseback. The state of my mind and course of life above indicated continued with me with but little variation until I reached my eighteenth year, except that I had then acquired an apetite [sic] for liquor, which I regret to say was indulged to excess too frequently for nearly five years, these were the saddest years of my life, conscious I was on the downward road to destruction, and yet impotent to stem the torrent of my impetuous inclination to drink.

I was, it seemed to me "of all men most miserable." Having passed my nineteenth year my mother died, that was a severe trial to me, and stopped me from a short time in my mad career. But unhappily even this was of short duration ere I was again going the downward way, yet notwithstanding all my down goings and wanderings, and in my darkest hours there remained a hope that one day I should cease from my evil ways, repent and turn unto God. That hope I am glad to know and believe was born of God otherwise it would never have been realized, therefore to Him be the glory. During these unhappy and yet momentous days of my life the Washington Temperance Society was organized, and meetings were then being held and auxilliary societies formed in almost every School District throughout the whole land. And accordingly a meeting for this purpose was announced to be held in Finesville in the month of April 1842. About this time I was seriously contemplating a reformation in my drinking habits. Learning of this meeting to be held at Finesville I gave the matter of a reformation more serious consideration than I had ever given it before, and finally reached an Iron Clad determination to attend that meeting and join the Society, which I did. I hesitated somewhat about signing the pledge, but some influential person present thought I had better do so as it would doubtless help me to stand more surely, besides setting a good example for others to follow, so I took the pledge too. Probably it was the means of helping me some; but I have always felt about the matter as Jonah did when the great fish picked him up from the depths of the sea and landed him on the shore; Jonah might have said the whale saved him, saved him, but he did not, he said "Salvation is of the Lord" and I have always felt it was the Lord who saved me from the drunkards doom. In the following winter of 1843 I attended a four days meeting held at Finesville conducted by Rev. Dr. Junkin. I cannot now remember that I was seriously impressed at any of its services until the closing sentences of the closing sermon when the Doctor paused a moment, looked up at me sitting in the farther end gallery of the old church and said "Rejoice O young man in thy youth, and let thine heart cheer thee in the days of thy youth, and walk in the ways of thine heart, and in the sight of thine eyes, but know thou, that for all these things, God will bring thee into judgement [sic]." These words came to me with power and in demonstration of the Spirit, convincing and convicting of sin of righteousness and of a judgement [sic] to come that made me quake and fear as I had never done before. However I said nothing to any one but came quietly and alone to my home, went to my bedroom and knelt down to pray when and where I had the clearest and most impressive sense of a present personal God that I ever before or since have felt or experienced. And while I prayed for forgiveness of sins and a new heart, He seemed to say to me I am here and ready to do these things for you if you are ready to receive them, and I was going to say I am ready, when the old devil appeared and made a little speach [sic], though I did not then recognize him, he said "it was a dreadful sin to make a profession of religion and then fall away again, as that would make my last state worse than the first" had'nt [sic] I better first try and see whether I could live like a Christian should before going too far, and as his remark seemed both scriptural and reasonable I postponed the matter for two days though the postponement afterward proved to be for two years. But he that hath loved me, as I trust, with an everlasting love, and did not, would not take his loving kindness entirely from me, but followed me day by day with the spirits gracious callings, and convictions which often brought me upon my knees and made me cry for mercy. It should perhaps be stated here, that up to this time I knew nothing of the plan of salvation, as it is revealed in the gospel, and therefore it was that while I made several attempts and resolutions to live as a Christian should. Yet these being all made in my own strength, they soon came to naught. In the year 1844 I was engaged in teaching school in a house then standing on the Warren County side of the Muskenetcong [sic] creek, near John Riegel's paper mill and boarded with the family of Ralph Hunt. These being Christian people I found their place a pleasant and helpful home. Being ignorant of the gospel method of Salvation, as before stated, and regarding it as a matter of greatest importance, that I must be correct in doctrine, in order to be the right kind of a Christian, I now gave much attention to the study of Theology. In those days the New Testament was used in the public schools as a reader and as such I had become somewhat familiar with it, especially the gospels. But as yet had never paid any particular attention as to what it taught concerning the several doctrines of the church. From my earliest years I had listened to much discussion of the doctrine of the Trinity, so that my mind was very unsettled on that doctrine. About this time however a friend handed me an old book published by the Church of England, the name of which I have forgotten. In it the doctrine of the Trinity was very thoroughly discussed, and as most of the argument used in favor of it were quotations taken from the Scriptures, which upon examination were found to be correctly given, I could not help seeing the doctrine was plainly taught in the Bible. And as I was never very good at explaining away the plain obvious meaning of scripture texts I was compelled to let it stand and pass on to the next. But that I may not seem to be too tedious I will at once say that I also found in the Bible all the once hated doctrines of origional [sic] sin, total depravity, Salvation by grace alone, election, Final perseverence [sic] of the saints, and last of all "predestination" which I made up my mind should never be any part of my creed. However afterwards, like Thomas Scott finding my system of doctrines incomplete without it and also finding it most assuredly taught in the scriptures I accepted it and became a predestinarian too, and have ever since been proud of that doctrine. Having settled as well as I could these questions of doctrine, I found that my conviction of sin and condemnation under the law still pursued me, and I was unhappy and knew not what to do, as yet I did not know what faith is, except that I had come to have some little idea of its being in part at least, an act of trust. But what did help me most at this time was a practical use, as it were of one of my chosen doctrines, viz. that Christ is indeed our surety and bondsman, and stood in our low place, to answer our obligations to satisfy divine justice and the demands of the law for our offences, and did indeed His own self bear our sins in his own body on the tree. One day after dismissing school and having been miserable all the day beyond description, and feeling I could not go to my boarding place that night with such a burden upon me I set about praying with great earnestness and with a determination, if possible, to overcome. After many petitions and cries for help offered without obtaining relief I gave up and started homeward with the burden still upon me. Upon reaching about half way up Forge Lane I stepped to one side the road, leaned against the fence and fell again to praying for deliverance and it was there I first saw the light felt my sins forgiven and the burden of my heart rolled away. I went the rest of my journey homeward rejoicing and strange to say thought I should never sin again, O how glad I was. However I said nothing about it to any one that evening, but thought I would tell it next morning. When the morning came, the old devil, who appeared to have gotten up earlier than usual that morning came to me while yet in bed, and said I was not converted at all, that thing, said he, is'nt [sic] done as easy as you think or as that little matter that happened you last night might seem to indicate. Being all my life a weak timid sort of any way, I at once got a little frightened and began to have some doubt over it myself. But on a second thought I told the old fellow I believed I was converted, for the Holy Spirit seemed to bear witness to the fact. Still the old devil, the flesh and the world continued to worry me until I then had, and have since had many secret misgivings and doubts myself as to its reality, and whether or not after all it might be only a delusion with me. However I do not remember that I ever quite lost all hopes. I still continued to attend upon religious duties, such as prayer, the reading and hearing of the word of God preached with a goodly degree of regularity, though with various fluctuations of feelings, sometimes I had a pleasing hope that I was a Christian, a renewed person; and then again distressed with doubts and fears and felt that I was still in my sins, sometimes I thought I ought to tell the church my state of mind, and ask to be received into it, but never feeling myself quite good enough to unite with the church I said nothing. In 1846 I abandoned school teaching and changed my place of residence to Holland, where I engaged myself to Isaac G. Britton to work on his saw mill. Here I had less time to devote to religious duties than formerly, still I did not wholly neglect them. In the meantime I purchased "Scotts Commentary of the Bible" Memoirs of Wm Walter Lowrie and "Baxster's Saint's Rest", these books afforded me much help and comfort.

At this time Rev. Jonathan H. Sherwood was preaching in the school house nearby, where I attended his meetings, and being something of a singer I soon became his chorister. At this time the question of building a house of worship and organizing a Presbyterian Church was being agitated by the people of Holland, a project in which I soon became interested somewhat; and after its establishment became an almost assured fact, I postponed the matter of uniting with any church until this one should be organized. Meantime in the year 1848 I married a wife who like myself had for some time been feeling it her duty to join the church. In April 1849 we removed to Riegelsville, N.J. where we set up housekeeping. At that time there was no church at Riegelsville. But Rev. Dr. Bomberger a minister of the German Reformed Church at Easton came down once a month a preached for us in the School house. Rev. Dr. Junkin also preached monthly at Finesville, both the meetings we attended quite regularly. In the fall of 1849 the Holland house of worship was finished and dedicated and preaching thereafter continued in it, which we also attended. In April 1850 we again returned to Holland. And in June 30 same year, together with others we appeared before the session of Milford Presbyterian Churchthen sitting in the new house of worship of Holland and were then and there received into church membership, after which I settled into what I supposed might be a saved state. In which condition I have since remained, though I am often constrained to say that under the power of an indwelling law I am but barely saved if saved at all. Oh that the Lord may guide, direct and keep me unto himself and everlasting life. I have no goodness of my own, but for Christ's sake I hope to be numbered with the chosen ones, when He comes to gather His sons, and daughters from afar. To the trembling, troubled children of God, there is no question of such deep, and vital importance, as that which concerns the reality of that hope in Christ, on which rests their assurance of eternal life. While it is true that the word of the Lord, upon which their hope rests, is sure and steadfastly fixed in the heart of every one who knows the joyful sound. Yet the tribulations, doubts, and fears through which they often pass, causes them often seriously to enquire, whether they are indeed the children of God. There may have been once a time of rejoicing with them; but that time is past and gone, and they now walk in darkness and can see no light. But for the encouragement of such one thing they may know and that is if they ever were the children of God they are his yet. O how comforting is the thought, "The Lord knoweth them that are his, that he will never leave nor forsake them, neither is any able to pluck them out of his hand."

▓ Index of Illustrations ▓

▦ INDEX ▦

Names have been listed using the spellings as they appear in the articles. Please look for variations in spelling.

135

146

CPSIA information can be obtained at www.ICGtesting.com
Printed in the USA
LVOW081348310313

326846LV00003B/328/P

9 781300 278405